ILLINOIS

DMV EXAM

WORKBOOK

The Ultimate Guide with 400+ Questions, a
Detailed Study Plan, and Bonus Tools for
Exam Success

WHY THIS WORKBOOK WORKS   5

INTRODUCTION   7

Study Plan for Your Exam: A Step-by-Step Guide   9

Step 1: Obtain and Review the DMV Handbook   10

Step 2: Take a Baseline Practice Test   11

Step 3: Review Road Signs and Traffic Signals   12

Step 4: Take a Full-Length Timed Practice Test   13

Step 5: Revise Key Areas and Cheat Sheets   14

Step 6: Take a Final Practice Test   15

Step 7: Prepare for Test Day   16

Final Thoughts   16

THE ILLINOIS DRIVER'S HANDBOOK   17

BONUSES & RESOURCES   19

RESOURCES   19

1. Road Sign Flashcards   19

2. Top 100 FAQs Flashcards   20

3. Most Commonly Missed Test Questions   20

200 BONUS PRACTICE QUESTIONS   22

PRACTICE TEST 1   25

PRACTICE TEST 2   39

PRACTICE TEST 3   53

INTERACTIVE ROAD SIGNS FLASHCARDS   67

ROAD SIGNS   69

SIGNS AND SITUATIONS   95

FINES & LIMITS   107

DISTRACTED DRIVING TEST   111

DRINKING AND DRIVING TEST   119

MOCK TEST   127

A MESSAGE FROM THE DRIVING SCHOOL   139

ANSWER SHEET   141

  PRACTICE TEST 1   143

  PRACTICE TEST 2   149

  PRACTICE TEST 3   155

  ROAD SIGNS   161

  SIGNS AND SITUATIONS   167

  FINE & LIMITS   171

  DISTRACTED DRIVING   173

  DRINKING AND DRIVING   177

  MOCK TEST PRACTICE   181

WHY THIS WORKBOOK WORKS

Since our journey began, we've had the privilege of helping thousands of aspiring drivers prepare for their DMV exams. Over 10,000 test-takers have shared their experiences with us, and their feedback has been invaluable in shaping the strategies and resources you'll find in this workbook.

A common theme we've noticed is that many people approach the DMV exam feeling confident but ultimately unprepared, often missing key steps that could ensure their success. On the other hand, those who passed on their first attempt consistently followed a few proven strategies: they engaged in regular, focused practice, utilized a variety of study tools, and thoroughly familiarized themselves with the exam material.

This workbook is designed to replicate those successful strategies, giving you access to practice tests, flashcards, and guides that have helped countless others achieve their goal of obtaining a driver's license. By following the steps laid out in this book, you'll be setting yourself up for success—just like the thousands of test-takers who came before you.

But don't just take our word for it. Here's what some of our satisfied customers have to say:

Ashley Cooper, New Driver
★★★★★
"This book was exactly what I needed to prepare for my test. The practice questions are spot-on, mirroring the actual exam format, and the state-specific focus ensured I was studying all the right material. The explanations made everything so easy to understand, and the extra bonuses, like flashcards and the downloadable handbook, were incredibly helpful. This book isn't just a study guide—it's the best tool out there to help you pass your test with confidence."

Maria Sanchez, Parent of a Teenager

★★★★★

"Helping my son study for the DMV test felt overwhelming until we found this workbook. The questions are clear, the structure is logical, and the state-specific details are perfect for making sure he's learning exactly what he needs to know. The extra practice tests were a huge confidence booster, and I appreciated the 100 FAQs that answered all our lingering questions, also the study plan helped him focus and guided him through the process. This book truly is a one-stop-shop for passing the DMV exam."

John Lee, First-Time Test Taker

★★★★★

"I was really nervous about taking my driving test, but the workbook took the edge off. The practice questions and mock exams were incredibly realistic, and the book's layout made studying so much more manageable. The state-specific focus meant I was getting the exact info I needed, and the added extras like the handbook download were super useful. I couldn't have asked for a better resource to get me ready."

Remember, the key to passing your DMV exam isn't just confidence—it's preparation. With the right approach, you can avoid the pitfalls that catch so many others off guard and join the ranks of those who have passed their exam with flying colors.

INTRODUCTION

Welcome, and thank you for choosing our workbook as your trusted companion on the journey to earning your driver's license. This carefully crafted resource is designed not just as a book but as a comprehensive guide that empowers you with the knowledge, confidence, and practice necessary to excel on your DMV test.

Each question in this workbook is thoughtfully selected and derived directly from your state's Driver's Manual, ensuring that you are studying the most relevant and accurate material. Our goal is to help you fully understand the concepts, so you can turn any uncertainties into strengths, ultimately leading to success on test day.

To get the most out of this workbook, we encourage you to adopt the following general strategies:

1. **Follow the Study Plan:** This workbook includes a detailed study plan designed to guide you step by step through your preparation. By adhering to this plan, you'll ensure that you cover all the necessary material systematically, avoiding any last-minute cramming. The study plan is structured to help you build your knowledge progressively, reinforce what you've learned, and track your progress along the way.
2. **Consistent Practice:** Regular practice is key to retaining information and building your test-taking endurance. Start by taking the practice tests under conditions that closely mimic the actual exam—one sitting, timed, and without interruptions. This will not only assess your current knowledge but also help you get comfortable with the format and timing of the real exam.
3. **Thorough Review:** After completing each practice test, spend time reviewing the questions you answered incorrectly. The answer key, located at the back of the book, provides detailed explanations for each question. Understanding your mistakes is crucial for improvement, as it allows you to correct misunderstandings and reinforces the correct information.
4. **Regular Revision:** To solidify your knowledge, make a habit of revisiting the material periodically. Regular revision helps

reinforce what you've learned and improves your ability to recall information during the exam. Remember, repetition is a powerful tool in the learning process.

5. **Stay Informed:** Driving laws and regulations can change, so it's important to ensure that you're studying the most up-to-date information. While this workbook is current, we recommend periodically checking online resources or contacting your local DMV to confirm there have been no recent changes to the laws in your state.

Remember, success is achieved through persistent and smart preparation. The more you engage with the material, the better you'll understand it, and the more confident you'll be when it's time to take the actual DMV exam.

Each question in this workbook is accompanied by a detailed explanation. In cases where multiple answers may seem correct, we've provided comprehensive explanations to clarify why the correct answer is right and why the others are not. This level of understanding is crucial—it's what differentiates those who merely pass from those who truly excel.

We believe that with dedication, practice, and the right guidance, you can master the skills required to pass the DMV test. This workbook is your roadmap to success. Follow the plan, put in the effort, and you'll be well on your way to becoming a confident and responsible driver.

Good luck on your journey!

Study Plan for Your Exam: A Step-by-Step Guide

Whether you're just starting or refining your knowledge before test day, this step-by-step guide will help you stay organized, focused, and on track. This plan breaks down the preparation process into manageable steps, ensuring that you cover all the essential material and build a solid foundation for success.

By following this guide, you'll be able to track your progress, identify areas where you need extra practice, and approach your exam with the confidence that comes from thorough preparation.

Let's get started on the road to acing your DMV exam!

Step 1: Obtain and Review the DMV Handbook

- **Objective:** Gain a thorough understanding of your state's traffic laws and regulations to form the foundation of your study plan.

- **Action Items:**
  - **Download or Pick Up the DMV Handbook:** Obtain the latest version of your state's DMV handbook. This is your primary study resource, covering all the rules, regulations, and road signs you need to know. You will find both a link and a QR code to download the **OFFICIAL** handbook on the next pages.
  - **Read Through the Handbook:** Schedule dedicated time to read through the entire handbook. It's best to break this into manageable sections (e.g., one chapter per day).
  - **Highlight Key Points:** As you read, use a highlighter or make notes in the margins to mark important information, such as speed limits, right-of-way rules, and specific state regulations.
  - **Create Summary Notes:** After reading each section, summarize the key points in your own words. This will reinforce your learning and create a quick reference guide for later review.

- **Progress Tracking:**
- Handbook obtained.
- Completed reading each section of the handbook.
- Highlighted key information.
- Created summary notes for quick reference.

Step 2: Take a Baseline Practice Test

- **Objective:** Establish a starting point by assessing your current knowledge and identifying areas that need improvement.

- **Action Items:**
  - **Complete the First 2 Practice Tests:** Set aside time to take the first 2 practice tests in the workbook. Ensure you simulate real test conditions by timing yourself and avoiding any outside help.
  - **Review Your Results:** After completing the test, carefully review your answers. Identify which questions you got wrong and understand why the correct answers are correct.
  - **Identify Weak Areas:** Make a list of the topics or question types where you struggled the most. This list will guide your focused study sessions in the next steps.

- **Progress Tracking:**
- Baseline practice tests completed.
- Results reviewed and analyzed.
- Weak areas identified.

Step 3: Review Road Signs and Traffic Signals

- **Objective:** Ensure that you can recognize and understand all road signs and traffic signals, which are crucial components of the DMV test.

- **Action Items:**
  - **Flashcards:** Practice with the online flashcards with images of road signs on one side and their meanings on the other. You can find the **link to the flashcards** in the Road Sign section and in the resources page.
  - **Study the Road Signs Section in the Workbook:** Carefully review the 50 questions and their explanations in the workbook's Road Signs and Signs and Situations sections to ensure you fully understand the meanings of all road signs.
  - **Practice Recognition:** Look for opportunities to identify road signs while driving or walking around your neighborhood. This real-world practice can reinforce what you've learned.

- **Progress Tracking:**
- Road Signs and Traffic Signals sections studied.
- Flashcards regularly reviewed.
- Real-world practice conducted.

Step 4: Take a Full-Length Timed Practice Test

- **Objective:** Simulate the real test environment to assess your readiness under pressure and ensure you're comfortable with the time constraints, by now you should have a solid understanding of key concepts.

- **Action Items:**
    - **Complete All Remaining Sections of the Workbook:** Make sure to work through any remaining sections of the workbook besides the Practice Test 3 and the Mock Test
    - **Complete Practice Test 3 Under Realistic Conditions:** Approach this practice test as if it were the real DMV exam. Avoid using any aids, and closely monitor your time. This will help you build test-taking stamina and get used to managing time effectively.
    - **Analyze Your Performance:** After completing the test, carefully review your answers to identify any mistakes. Pay special attention to the questions you answered incorrectly or felt uncertain about.

Progress Tracking:

- All remaining workbook sections completed.
- Full-length timed practice test 3 completed.
- Test results reviewed and analyzed.

Step 5: Revise Key Areas and Cheat Sheets

- **Objective:** Refresh your knowledge on the most critical topics, ensuring they are top of mind as your test date approaches.

- **Action Items:**
  - **Top 100 Most Frequently Asked Questions:** Access this resource and review each question thoroughly. These are the questions that appear most often on the test, so becoming familiar with them will increase your chances of success.
  - **Commonly Missed Test Questions:** This section highlights the questions that test-takers often get wrong. By studying these questions, you'll be better prepared to tackle tricky items and avoid common mistakes on the exam.
  - **Revisit Important Sections of the Handbook:** Focus on revising key topics such as speed limits, right-of-way rules, and other essential regulations.
  - **Review Practice Test Mistakes:** Go over the mistakes you made in your practice tests. Ensure you understand why you got them wrong and what the correct answers are.
  - **Final Study Session:** Schedule a dedicated study session a few days before the test to go over all your notes, summaries, and practice questions one last time.

- **Progress Tracking:**
- Important handbook sections revised.
- Practice test mistakes reviewed.
- Final study session completed.
- Top 100 FAQs
- Commonly Missed Test Questions

Step 6: Take a Final Practice Test

- **Objective:** Confirm your readiness by taking one last practice test to ensure you're fully prepared for the actual exam.

- **Action Items:**
  - **Take the Mock Test:** Instead of choosing a random practice test, take the mock test provided in your study resources. Complete it under timed conditions to simulate the actual exam experience.
  - **Aim for 90% or Higher:** Strive to score at least 90% on this final test. This will give you a comfortable margin of error for the actual exam.
  - **Review Any Remaining Weaknesses:** If there are still areas where you're scoring low, take some extra time to review these topics before the exam.
  - **Bonus Questions:** If your score is still below 80%, we recommend downloading the 200 Bonus Questions for additional practice and reinforcement.

- **Progress Tracking:**
- Final practice test completed.
- Achieved target score (90% or higher).
- Remaining weak areas reviewed.

Step 7: Prepare for Test Day

- **Objective:** Ensure you are fully prepared both mentally and logistically for the DMV test.

- **Action Items:**
  - **Get Plenty of Rest:** Make sure to get a good night's sleep before the test day.
  - **Stay Calm and Confident:** On the day of the test, take a few deep breaths, review any key points you feel unsure about, and trust in your preparation.
  - **Review Key Resources:** If time permits, go over the *Top 100 Most Frequently Asked Questions* and *Commonly Missed Test Questions.*
  - **The day before your exam:** Make sure to read the concise guide, "*8 Tips for Guaranteed Success on Your Driving Test*" This resource is packed with practical advice designed to boost your confidence.

- **Progress Tracking:**
- Adequate rest before the test.
- Arrived at the DMV on time and fully prepared.
- Revise the Top 100 FAQs and Commonly Missed Test Questions
- Read the short guide on "8 Tips for Guaranteed Success on Your Driving Test"

Final Thoughts

This detailed study plan is designed to guide you through every step of your DMV exam preparation, ensuring that you're fully equipped to succeed. By following this plan and tracking your progress along the way, you'll build confidence and mastery over the material, setting yourself up for a successful test day.

Remember, consistent effort and focused study are the keys to passing your DMV exam on the first attempt. Good luck!

THE ILLINOIS DRIVER'S HANDBOOK

The Illinois Department of Motor Vehicles strongly recommends that all test takers familiarize themselves with the official manual. This comprehensive guide offers an in-depth understanding of the rules, regulations, and knowledge required to pass your exam. It is suggested that you read through this manual at least once to familiarize yourself with the necessary content.

To access this invaluable resource, simply scan the provided QR code or type the link into your browser to download it.

https://www.ilsos.gov/publications/pdf_publications/dsd_a112.pdf

Additional Study Resources

To further support your preparation, we've included a suite of bonus resources that go beyond the official handbook. These tools are designed to enhance your study experience and help you feel fully prepared on test day. On the next page, you'll find QR codes and links to access the following:

- **Road Sign Flashcards:** An interactive tool to help you master the road signs you'll encounter on the exam.
- **Top 100 FAQs Flashcards:** Flashcards covering the most frequently asked questions on the DMV test.

- **Most Commonly Missed Test Questions:** A guide to the questions that often trip up test-takers, helping you avoid common mistakes.
- **"8 Tips to Pass and You'll Pass. Guaranteed!" Guide:** A practical guide with proven tips to help you pass your DMV exam on the first try.

Simply scan the QR codes or type in your browser the links to access these resources instantly. If you encounter any issues or have questions, feel free to reach out to us at **info@infiniteinkpress.org**—we're here to help!

Your Journey to Success

We are dedicated to helping you succeed in obtaining your driver's license. To maximize your chances of passing the DMV exam, we encourage you to take full advantage of the practice tests and resources provided in this workbook. Consistent practice and thorough review of the material are key to mastering the content and boosting your confidence.

Now is the perfect time to dive into your studies and start your journey toward acing the DMV exam! We're honored that you've chosen this book as your guide, and we're confident that it will help you achieve your driving goals.

Finally, we'd love to hear about your experience with this book. Your feedback is invaluable in helping us improve our resources and better assist future drivers. Please consider leaving a review and sharing your thoughts on your learning journey.

Good luck, and happy studying!

BONUSES & RESOURCES

RESOURCES

We're committed to providing you with the tools and resources you need to succeed on your DMV exam. Below, you'll find links and QR codes to access our exclusive online bonuses, designed to enhance your study experience and boost your confidence as you prepare for the test.

1. Road Sign Flashcards

Mastering road signs is essential for both the written and practical parts of your DMV exam. Our interactive Road Sign Flashcards are designed to help you quickly and effectively learn and retain the meanings of various road signs.

- **Access the Road Sign Flashcards:**
  expert-driving-school.webflow.io

2. Top 100 FAQs Flashcards

We've compiled the top 100 most frequently asked questions on the DMV exam and turned them into flashcards to help you test your knowledge and ensure you're ready for any question that might come your way.

- **Access the Top 100 FAQs Flashcards:**
  expert-driving-school.webflow.io/flashcards-dmv-questions

3. Most Commonly Missed Test Questions

Avoid common pitfalls with our guide to the Most Commonly Missed Test Questions. This resource will help you focus on the areas where test-takers typically struggle, giving you an advantage on exam day.

- **Access the Most Commonly Missed Test Questions:**
  https://bit.ly/Missed-Questions

4. "8 Tips for Guaranteed Success on Your Driving Test!" Guide

Our "8 Tips for Guaranteed Success on Your Driving Test" guide is packed with practical advice and proven strategies to help you ace your DMV exam. Follow these tips, and you'll set yourself up for success.

- **Access the "8 Tips for Guaranteed Success on Your Driving Test" Guide:**
  https://bit.ly/DMV-Guaranteed

200 BONUS PRACTICE QUESTIONS

"Bonus Practice Questions" is a comprehensive collection of additional, carefully crafted questions that mirror the variety, style, and complexity of the ones you'll encounter in the real DMV exam. Perhaps you've already completed the questions in our main guide and are yearning for more practice. Or maybe you just want to challenge yourself and ensure no stone is left unturned in your preparations. Regardless of your motivation, this bonus eBook is your perfect ally.

To retrieve this resource, simply enter the provided link into your browser or make use of the QR Code for swift access.

https://dl.bookfunnel.com/l15oxwpd9e

How to Use These Resources

- **Scan the QR Codes:** Simply point your smartphone camera at the QR code for instant access to the resource. This feature is especially useful if you're on the go.
- **Click the Links:** If you're reading this on a digital device, you can click the hyperlinks to be taken directly to the resources.
- **Bookmark the Pages:** Save the links in your browser or add them to your favorites so you can return to these valuable tools whenever you need a quick review.

If you encounter any problem, please send us an email at **info@infiniteinkpress.org** we will be happy to help you!

PRACTICE TEST 1

Prepare for the DMV driving permit test by practicing with questions that closely resemble (and are almost identical to) those you'll encounter on the actual DMV exam. We strongly recommend that you go through each question, time yourself, and only review your answers after completing the entire practice test. The answers can be found in the last section of the book.

Total Questions: 40
Correct Answer to pass: 32

Question 1 - Practice Test 1

When accessing a main road from a private driveway, road, or alleyway, you must _____.

- ☐ stop entirely and yield the right of way to pedestrians, bicyclists, or vehicles on the road you are entering
- ☐ slowly approach and then yield to pedestrians, bicyclists, or vehicles on the road you're merging onto
- ☐ stop fully and make a left turn onto the road you're merging onto
- ☐ halt entirely and make a right turn onto the road you're merging onto

Question 2 - Practice Test 1

If the traffic lights are malfunctioning at an intersection, you must _____ before advancing through the intersection.

- ☐ change your lane
- ☐ stop entirely
- ☐ slow your speed
- ☐ speed up

Question 3 - Practice Test 1

When changing lanes, about to overtake another vehicle, or merging into traffic, use your signal and check for overtaking traffic. Start by looking at your mirrors. Then

- ☐ inspect the back of your vehicle
- ☐ verify your vehicle's blind spot
- ☐ look at the front of your vehicle
- ☐ watch for approaching traffic

Question 4 - Practice Test 1

Upon entering an interstate highway from an acceleration lane, you are required to _____.

- ☐ stop and wait for an opening to merge
- ☐ reduce your speed
- ☐ match the speed of highway traffic or adhere to the posted legal speed limit
- ☐ increase your speed above the posted speed limit for merging

Question 5 - Practice Test 1

When driving on a one-way street with three or more traffic lanes, you should use _____.

- ☐ the outside lanes for through travel and turning
- ☐ the outside lanes for through travel and the middle lanes for turning
- ☐ the outside lanes for turning and the middle lanes for through travel
- ☐ the middle lanes for through travel and turning

Question 6 - Practice Test 1

Which of the following statements about overtaking a vehicle is incorrect?

- ☐ You may go over the legal speed limit to pass quickly

- ☐ You should avoid overtaking more than one vehicle at a time

- ☐ Do not trail another vehicle that is overtaking a car ahead of you

- ☐ Typically, you should overtake on the left

Question 7 - Practice Test 1

If another vehicle is overtaking you, you should _____.

- ☐ shift into the left lane

- ☐ increase your speed

- ☐ move your vehicle to the right and refrain from increasing your speed

- ☐ maintain your lane and avoid speeding up

Question 8 - Practice Test 1

On a multi-lane road, _____ adjacent to your lane signify(s) that you are permitted to overtake when it is safe.

- ☐ a solid white line

- ☐ a solid yellow line

- ☐ two solid yellow lines

- ☐ a dashed white line

Question 9 - Practice Test 1

When you observe a pedestrian crossing at an unmarked crosswalk where there are no traffic signals, you should _____.

☐   give right of way to the pedestrian

☐   proceed slowly as there are no traffic signals

☐   engage your hazard lights and cautiously continue

☐   alert the pedestrian and cautiously proceed

Question 10 - Practice Test 1

Diagonal yellow stripes on roads and highways suggest that

☐   a) the road is narrowing

☐   b) there is an obstruction on the roadway

☐   neither a) nor b)

☐   either a) or b)

Question 11 - Practice Test 1

If you need to check a map or directions while driving, _____.

☐   lower your driving speed and take a look at the map

☐   try to glimpse it briefly while continuing to drive

☐   halt your vehicle on the street to study the map

☐   identify a safe spot, pull over, and stop the car to read the map

Question 12 - Practice Test 1

When driving at night, when should you use your high-beam headlights?

☐   Within city limits

☐   When you're on an open country road with no other vehicles nearby

☐   While driving under the influence of alcohol

☐   While on a highway

Question 13 - Practice Test 1

If dense fog descends while you're driving, reducing visibility almost to zero, what should you do?

☐   Safely pull as far off the road as you can and stop

☐   Switch to high-beam headlights

☐   Switch to low-beam headlights

☐   Reduce your speed and find a detour

Question 14 - Practice Test 1

Which of the following behaviors indicate road rage?

☐   Tailgating

☐   Forcing a car off the road

☐   Excessive honking

☐   All of the above

Question 15 - Practice Test 1

If you are preparing to pass a cyclist on your right and an oncoming vehicle is approaching from your left, you should

    ☐   slow down and allow the vehicle to pass first

    ☐   drive between the incoming vehicle and the cyclist

    ☐   stop your vehicle on the shoulder

    ☐   accelerate and pass the cyclist quickly

Question 16 - Practice Test 1

At an intersection, a steady yellow arrow pointing left indicates

    ☐   oncoming traffic is stopped

    ☐   the yellow arrow is about to turn red

    ☐   you should increase your speed

    ☐   none of the above

Question 17 - Practice Test 1

Never make a U-turn on a bend or near the crest of a hill if you are not visible to _____.

    ☐   the drivers who have stopped on the roadside

    ☐   the drivers approaching from both directions

    ☐   the drivers ahead of you

    ☐   the drivers to your right

Question 18 - Practice Test 1

In order to prevent panic stops, you need to

☐ brake rapidly

☐ spot potential hazards well ahead of time

☐ follow other vehicles closely

☐ change lanes swiftly

Question 19 - Practice Test 1

The vision test for obtaining a driver's license evaluates _____.

☐ depth perception and color recognition

☐ side vision

☐ visual clarity

☐ all of the above

Question 20 - Practice Test 1

To avoid highway hypnosis on an expressway, you should _____.

☐ constantly chat on your mobile phone

☐ continually move your eyes around different areas of the roadway

☐ listen to extremely loud music

☐ continually switch between lanes

Question 21 - Practice Test 1

While turning a corner, which technique should you utilize to turn the steering wheel?

- ☐ the single-hand technique
- ☐ the hand-to-hand technique
- ☐ the hand-over-hand technique
- ☐ the two-hand technique

Question 22 - Practice Test 1

A pedestrian who is carrying a white cane, possibly tipped with red, is typically _____.

- ☐ a student
- ☐ a crew member
- ☐ a flag bearer (flagger)
- ☐ blind

Question 23 - Practice Test 1

On an expressway entrance ramp, a _____ sign indicates that you're heading in the wrong direction.

- ☐ Do Not Enter
- ☐ One Way Ahead
- ☐ Road Closed Ahead
- ☐ Detour

Question 24 - Practice Test 1

If your brakes malfunction while driving, you should not _____.

- ☐   shift down to a lower gear to decrease speed
- ☐   stop your vehicle by colliding with a solid object
- ☐   gradually apply the parking or emergency brake
- ☐   pump the brake pedal to regain brake pressure

Question 25 - Practice Test 1

When is it permissible to drive on the road's shoulder to overtake another vehicle?

- ☐   Never
- ☐   When the vehicle is turning right
- ☐   When the vehicle is halted due to an emergency
- ☐   When the vehicle is turning left

Question 26 - Practice Test 1

What should be avoided when traversing railroad tracks?

- ☐   Stopping or changing gears
- ☐   Using high-beam headlights
- ☐   Applying brakes
- ☐   Using low-beam headlights

Question 27 - Practice Test 1

While waiting to turn left at an intersection, the traffic light turns yellow. What should you do?

- ☐ Turn right instead
- ☐ Proceed straight, then execute a U-turn
- ☐ Turn left
- ☐ Stay halted in the intersection until the light turns green in your favor

Question 28 - Practice Test 1

When overtaking another vehicle, you must pass on the left at a safe distance and NOT _____ until the way is clear.

- ☐ speed up
- ☐ continue straight
- ☐ re-enter the original lane
- ☐ return to the passing lane

Question 29 - Practice Test 1

If a driver behind you consistently flashes his or her headlights, you should _____.

- ☐ increase your speed and move ahead
- ☐ turn on your low-beam headlights
- ☐ turn on your high-beam headlights
- ☐ move out of the way

If you start to skid, what should you do?

☐ Immediately apply the brakes and sharply steer away from the direction you want the car to go

☐ Ease your foot off the gas and carefully steer away from the direction you want the car to go

☐ Ease your foot off the gas and carefully steer in the direction of the skid

☐ Immediately apply the brakes and carefully steer in the direction you want the car to go

Question 31 - Practice Test 1

When executing a 'Zipper Merge', you should

☐ reach the point of lane closure and then take turns with other drivers to join the remaining lane

☐ speed up and use the shoulder to merge if there's no space

☐ merge into the open lane at the earliest opportunity

☐ get to the lane reduction point and merge at that spot, assuming you have right of way

Question 32 - Practice Test 1

Which of the following can be considered a legal spot for parking?

☐ Within 30 feet of a traffic signal, yield sign, or stop sign

☐ On a bridge, overpass, in a tunnel, or underpass

☐ On a crosswalk or sidewalk

☐ At the curb or edge of a public road

Question 33 - Practice Test 1

Which of the following statements about parking is incorrect?

- ☐ It's illegal to park on a freeway
- ☐ In emergencies, it's permissible to park on the shoulder of the road, as far from traffic as possible
- ☐ When parking on a downhill grade, you should turn your wheels toward the curb
- ☐ It's legal to park within 15 feet of a fire hydrant

Question 34 - Practice Test 1

When you approach pedestrians, who are walking on or crossing the road, you should

- ☐ speed up and move quickly
- ☐ slow down, yield, and be ready to stop
- ☐ turn on your emergency lights
- ☐ honk your horn, slow down, and stop

Question 35 - Practice Test 1

When stopped behind another vehicle on a slope, you should keep at least _____.

- ☐ two vehicle lengths
- ☐ three vehicle lengths
- ☐ four vehicle lengths
- ☐ one vehicle length

Question 36 - Practice Test 1

Which of the following statements about lane markings is accurate?

☐   A broken yellow line between opposite lanes of traffic means you are not permitted to cross the line

☐   A solid white line alongside your lane means you should remain in your lane unless a special situation necessitates a lane change

☐   Where there are both a solid and a dashed yellow line between opposing lanes of traffic, you are allowed to overtake if the solid line is on your side

☐   Double solid yellow lines between opposite lanes of traffic mean either side can overtake

Question 37 - Practice Test 1

It's never advised to drive alongside a motorcycle in the same lane because _____.

☐   the motorcyclist might lead you astray

☐   motorcycles need the entire lane width

☐   motorcyclists are exempt from traffic rules

☐   motorcycles lack signal lights

Question 38 - Practice Test 1

When making a left turn at an intersection, alley, or driveway, you must give way to _____.

☐   all traffic to your vehicle's right

☐   all traffic behind your vehicle

☐   all traffic moving in the same direction

☐   all traffic coming from the opposite direction

Question 39 - Practice Test 1

If you wish to enter a freeway, you should _____.

- ☐ stop and yield to the traffic already on the freeway
- ☐ enter the freeway at a minimal speed
- ☐ come to a halt before merging with freeway traffic
- ☐ get on the freeway at a speed that matches or is close to the speed of freeway traffic

Question 40 - Practice Test 1

On a multi-lane road with several lanes in one direction, you should use _____ for overtaking.

- ☐ any lane
- ☐ the middle lane
- ☐ the middle and left lanes
- ☐ the right lane

PRACTICE TEST 2

We strongly recommend that you go through each question, time yourself, and only review your answers after completing the entire practice test. The answers can be found in the last section of the book.

Total Questions: 40
Correct Answer to pass: 32

Question 1 - Practice Test 2

On a hot day, if it begins to rain, be aware that the pavement can become slippery initially. What causes this?

- ☐ Oil from the car
- ☐ Melting of the tires
- ☐ Moisture within the asphalt
- ☐ Oil within the asphalt

Question 2 - Practice Test 2

If a driver has their hand and arm bent at a 90-degree angle and pointing downward, what does it signal?

- ☐ They're about to make a right turn
- ☐ They're slowing down or planning to stop
- ☐ They're going straight
- ☐ They're making a left turn

Question 3 - Practice Test 2

If your vehicle's engine fails while you're maneuvering a curve, what should you do?

☐   Try to restart the engine while on the road

☐   Firmly grip the steering wheel and maintain a straight path

☐   Reduce pressure on the gas pedal

☐   Steer to the right side of the road

Question 4 - Practice Test 2

What offers the best protection in a car crash and serves as the most effective shield against a drunk driver?

☐   A cushion seat

☐   A toolkit

☐   A safety belt

☐   A windshield wiper

Question 5 - Practice Test 2

Why are rear-end collisions a common occurrence on highways?

☐   Drivers often take too long to apply the brakes

☐   Drivers follow too closely

☐   Drivers are under the influence of alcohol

☐   Drivers fail to use their headlights

Question 6 - Practice Test 2

If an oncoming vehicle is in your lane, how can you avoid a head-on collision?

- ☐ Steer left toward the median
- ☐ Keep the steering wheel straight
- ☐ Steer right toward the shoulder or curb line
- ☐ Accelerate

Question 7 - Practice Test 2

A roundabout is a circular intersection in which vehicles travel around a center island in the following direction:

- ☐ Clockwise
- ☐ In a straight line
- ☐ Counterclockwise
- ☐ Any direction

Question 8 - Practice Test 2

What should you do when getting ready to exit a parallel parking spot?

- ☐ Signal your intentions
- ☐ Check your mirrors
- ☐ Look over your shoulder
- ☐ All of the above

Question 9 - Practice Test 2

In the event that your vehicle breaks down on train tracks with a train approaching, what is the appropriate course of action?

- ☐ Alert the train by opening your doors and signaling

- ☐ Quickly evacuate the vehicle and move a safe distance away

- ☐ Attempt to restart the engine

- ☐ Make an effort to push the vehicle off the tracks

Question 10 - Practice Test 2

When double solid lines are present next to your lane, it means you are:

- ☐ Not permitted to pass or change lanes

- ☐ Permitted to pass

- ☐ Allowed to change lanes

- ☐ Allowed to make a turn

Question 11 - Practice Test 2

In heavy rain, your car's tires can lose contact with the road by riding on a layer of water. This is known as:

- ☐ Waterplaning

- ☐ Rainplaning

- ☐ Frictionplaning

- ☐ Hydroplaning

Question 12 - Practice Test 2

When two vehicles encounter each other on a steep mountain road where neither can pass, which vehicle has the right-of-way?

- ☐ Neither of the vehicles
- ☐ The vehicle descending the hill
- ☐ The vehicle ascending the hill
- ☐ The vehicle that arrives first

Question 13 - Practice Test 2

Avoiding panic stops can be achieved by _____.

- ☐ quickly changing lanes
- ☐ applying brakes abruptly
- ☐ identifying hazards well in advance
- ☐ following other vehicles closely

Question 14 - Practice Test 2

If your gas pedal is stuck and you can't free it with your foot, you should _____.

- ☐ continue driving until the gas is depleted
- ☐ apply brakes forcefully
- ☐ switch to neutral gear
- ☐ dial 911 on your mobile phone

Question 15 - Practice Test 2

When you are driving down a steep hill, you should _____.

- ☐ switch to a higher gear
- ☐ switch to a lower gear
- ☐ continually apply the brakes
- ☐ activate your hazard lights

Question 16 - Practice Test 2

When driving on gravel or dirt, you must reduce your speed because _____.

- ☐ it's uncomfortable to drive fast
- ☐ your vehicle will accumulate more dirt at higher speeds
- ☐ you don't have much traction
- ☐ the dirt may obscure your windshield

Question 17 - Practice Test 2

If another driver is tailgating you, the best response is to _____.

- ☐ move to the right lane and stop
- ☐ move to the left lane and stop
- ☐ move to the right lane and reduce your speed
- ☐ move to the left lane and reduce your speed

Question 18 - Practice Test 2

Your braking distance increases by _____ times, if you double your speed on a highway.

- ☐ three
- ☐ two
- ☐ ten
- ☐ four

Question 19 - Practice Test 2

The practice of continually being aware of driving conditions, planning ahead, anticipating hazards, and taking appropriate actions to prevent collisions is known as _____.

- ☐ defensive driving
- ☐ good driving
- ☐ safe driving
- ☐ positive driving

Question 20 - Practice Test 2

When passing another vehicle, you must pass at a safe distance and should NOT _____ until the way is clear.

- ☐ continue in a straight line
- ☐ accelerate
- ☐ move back into the passing lane
- ☐ return to your original lane

Question 21 - Practice Test 2

Faster vehicles should use _____, on a highway with three or more lanes going in one direction.

- ☐ the exit ramp
- ☐ a middle lane
- ☐ the right lane
- ☐ the left lane

Question 22 - Practice Test 2

Your chances of surviving a car crash increase when you use _____ together.

- ☐ the lap belt and shoulder belt
- ☐ the lap belt and a helmet
- ☐ the shoulder belt and hazard flashers
- ☐ none of the above

Question 23 - Practice Test 2

When changing lanes, preparing to pass another vehicle, or merging into traffic, signal and check for passing traffic. First, use your mirrors, then _____.

- ☐ check your vehicle's blind spots
- ☐ inspect the rear of your vehicle
- ☐ check for oncoming traffic
- ☐ check the front of your vehicle

Question 24 - Practice Test 2

On a roadway with three or more lanes traveling in the same direction, which lanes generally offer the smoothest flow of traffic?

- ☐ Acceleration lanes
- ☐ Left lane
- ☐ Right lane
- ☐ Middle lanes

Question 25 - Practice Test 2

Backing up your vehicle in any travel lane should never be done EXCEPT _____.

- ☐ to parallel park
- ☐ at crossroads
- ☐ while making a U-turn
- ☐ at lane crossings

Question 26 - Practice Test 2

You should never drive in the same lane as a motorcycle. Why?

- ☐ The motorcycle requires the entire width of the lane
- ☐ Motorcyclists are not required to respect traffic laws
- ☐ Motorcycles do not have turn signals
- ☐ The motorcycle may lead you astray

Question 27 - Practice Test 2

Vertical rectangular signs with white backgrounds and black letters are typically used as:

- ☐ regulation signs
- ☐ facility signs
- ☐ caution signs
- ☐ directional signs

Question 28 - Practice Test 2

To make a right turn, look left and right, yield the right-of-way, and turn the steering wheel using the technique of:

- ☐ Hand-off-hand
- ☐ the one-handed technique
- ☐ the two-handed technique
- ☐ the hand-over-hand method

Question 29 - Practice Test 2

In which of the following scenarios are you not required to stop completely?

- ☐ When encountering a flashing red traffic light
- ☐ When encountering a stop sign
- ☐ When encountering a steady red traffic light
- ☐ When encountering a flashing yellow traffic light

Question 30 - Practice Test 2

Signs for work zones or construction zones usually have:

- ☐ black letters on an orange background.
- ☐ white letters on an orange background
- ☐ white letters on a yellow background
- ☐ black letters on a yellow background

Question 31 - Practice Test 2

In the event of a tire blowout while driving, you should:

- ☐ Accelerate
- ☐ Brake forcefully
- ☐ Shift to a higher gear
- ☐ Grip the steering wheel tightly

Question 32 - Practice Test 2

Where are car and motorcycle accidents most likely to occur?

- ☐ At roundabouts
- ☐ One-way roads
- ☐ Multi-lane highways
- ☐ At intersections

Question 33 - Practice Test 2

When is it permissible to pass another vehicle?

- ☐ When you are within 100 feet of a railroad crossing
- ☐ When a broken line is present in your lane
- ☐ When a school bus with flashing lights is on the same road
- ☐ On the right shoulder of the highway

Question 34 - Practice Test 2

What strategy should you employ to prevent a collision?

- ☐ Maintain a space cushion
- ☐ Stay on the left side of your lane
- ☐ Switch Lanes frequently
- ☐ Tailgate other vehicles

Question 35 - Practice Test 2

What is the most appropriate method to handle a curve?

- ☐ Slow down before entering the curve
- ☐ Gradually increase your speed before entering the curve
- ☐ Begin turning the vehicle just before the curve and quickly accelerate
- ☐ Stay on your side of the road and drive as far to the left as possible

Question 36 - Practice Test 2

When you approach a roundabout, you should always enter the _____ of the central island.

- ☐ center
- ☐ right
- ☐ corner
- ☐ left

Question 37 - Practice Test 2

What should you do if your brakes fail while you're driving and your vehicle doesn't have antilock brakes (ABS)?

- ☐ Switch into a lower gear
- ☐ Use the parking brake
- ☐ Pump the brake pedal
- ☐ Do all of the above

Question 38 - Practice Test 2

Typically, _____ are diamond-shaped with black letters or symbols on a yellow background.

- ☐ Warning signs
- ☐ Service signs
- ☐ Regulatory signs
- ☐ Destination signs

Question 39 - Practice Test 2

What can be used to guide drivers into specific traffic lanes in work zones during the day and night?

- ☐   Railroad crossing signals
- ☐   Large flashing or sequencing arrow panels
- ☐   Flag persons
- ☐   Barricades

Question 40 - Practice Test 2

At an intersection, a steady yellow traffic light signifies that you should:

- ☐   Accelerate to pass the signal before it turns red
- ☐   Slow down and proceed with caution
- ☐   Maintain your current speed
- ☐   Prepare to stop for a red light

PRACTICE TEST 3

We strongly recommend that you go through each question, time yourself, and only review your answers after completing the entire practice test. The answers can be found in the last section of the book.

Total Questions: 40
Correct Answer to pass: 32

Question 1 - Practice Test 3

A vehicle's stopping distance is the total distance it takes to stop, which is equal to:

☐ The combined distance of reaction time and following distance

☐ The distance traveled while braking

☐ The sum of braking distance and following distance

☐ The sum of reaction distance and braking distance

Question 2 - Practice Test 3

Vehicles approaching a roundabout should

☐ enter the roundabout at a speed of 35 mph

☐ enter the roundabout yielding to the traffic already inside

☐ enter the roundabout to the left of the central island

☐ come to a complete stop and wait for the roundabout traffic to clear

Question 3 - Practice Test 3

A double solid white line _____.

☐ indicates that crossing over is prohibited and separates lanes traveling in the same direction

☐ indicates that crossing over is permitted and separates lanes traveling in the same direction

☐ indicates that crossing over is prohibited and separates opposing lanes

☐ indicates that crossing over is permitted and separates opposing lanes

Question 4 - Practice Test 3

When driving on a one-way street with three or more lanes, you should use _____.

☐ the center lanes for straight driving and turning

☐ the outer lanes for turning and any lane for through travel

☐ the outer lanes for straight driving and the center lanes for turning

☐ any lane for making turns

Question 5 - Practice Test 3

You shouldn't pass _____.

☐ when there is a solid yellow line adjacent to your lane

☐ when approaching a hill or curve with limited visibility

☐ a school bus ahead displaying flashing red lights and an extended stop arm

☐ in any of the situations mentioned above

Question 6 - Practice Test 3

If there are no traffic signals, you should slow down or stop to yield to pedestrians at _____.

- ☐ an intersection
- ☐ an unmarked crosswalk
- ☐ a marked crosswalk
- ☐ all of the above

Question 7 - Practice Test 3

On steep mountain grades, _____ are constructed to safely stop runaway vehicles without causing harm to drivers or passengers.

- ☐ weave lanes
- ☐ escape ramps
- ☐ deceleration lanes
- ☐ acceleration lanes

Question 8 - Practice Test 3

If a driver behind you repeatedly flashes their headlights, you must _____.

- ☐ turn on your low-beam headlights
- ☐ turn on your high-beam headlights
- ☐ move out of the way
- ☐ increase your speed and move forward

Question 9 - Practice Test 3

Which scenario is not advisable for passing another vehicle?

- ☐ When the road markings are dashed yellow lines
- ☐ When the road markings are dashed white lines
- ☐ When the vehicle ahead is moving slower than the safe speed
- ☐ When you're moving through an intersection

Question 10 - Practice Test 3

Which of the following assertions is incorrect?

- ☐ Increase your following distance when driving around bicycles
- ☐ Motorcycles are entitled to the same full lane width as other vehicles
- ☐ Never drive next to a motorcycle in the same lane
- ☐ Bicycles and motorcycles move slower and stop slower than expected.

Question 11 - Practice Test 3

If your vehicle's rear wheels begin to skid, what should you do?

- ☐ Steer the wheel to the left
- ☐ Steer the wheel in the direction of the skid
- ☐ Steer the wheel opposite the skid
- ☐ Steer the wheel to the right

When two vehicles approach an intersection from opposite directions at approximately the same time, who has the right-of-way?

- ☐ The left-turning vehicle must yield to the vehicle going straight or turning right
- ☐ The vehicle with more passengers should go first
- ☐ The vehicle on the right must yield to the vehicle on the left
- ☐ The right-turning vehicle must yield to the left-turning vehicle

Question 13 - Practice Test 3

When entering a roundabout, rotary, or traffic circle, you must yield the right-of-way to:

- ☐ Pedestrians
- ☐ Both pedestrians and vehicles already in the circle
- ☐ Vehicles in the circle
- ☐ Nobody

Question 14 - Practice Test 3

For improved visibility in fog, rain, or snow, use:

- ☐ Emergency lights
- ☐ Low-beam headlights
- ☐ High-beam headlights
- ☐ Interior lights

Question 15 - Practice Test 3

You shall not pass a vehicle on the left if:

- ☐ Your lane has a broken white line
- ☐ Your lane has a solid yellow centerline
- ☐ You are far away from a curve
- ☐ Your lane has a broken yellow line

Question 16 - Practice Test 3

_____ enable vehicles to exit expressways.

- ☐ Exit ramps
- ☐ Turnpikes
- ☐ Acceleration lanes
- ☐ Roundabouts

Question 17 - Practice Test 3

To perform a turnaround on a narrow, two-way street, execute:

- ☐ Single-point turn
- ☐ Two-point turn
- ☐ Four-point turn
- ☐ Three-point turn

Question 18 - Practice Test 3

Even ____ alcoholic drink(s) can impact your ability to drive safely.

- ☐ three
- ☐ four
- ☐ one
- ☐ two

Question 19 - Practice Test 3

When another vehicle passes you on the left, you should _____ until the vehicle has safely overtaken you.

☐   pull over and stop

☐   accelerate and keep to the right

☐   slow down and stay to the left

☐   slow down and stay centered in your lane

Question 20 - Practice Test 3

When turning right on a multi-lane road, which lane should you typically use?

☐   Any lane

☐   The leftmost lane

☐   A middle lane

☐   The rightmost lane

Question 21 - Practice Test 3

When is it prohibited to pass a vehicle on the right?

☐   When the vehicle is making a left turn

☐   When the vehicle is going straight

☐   When the vehicle is making a right turn

☐   When the vehicle is on a one-way road with two lanes of traffic

Question 22 - Practice Test 3

In open country at night, which headlights should you use?

- ☐ High-beam headlights
- ☐ Parking lights
- ☐ Low-beam headlights
- ☐ None of the above

Question 23 - Practice Test 3

Due to their size, tractor-trailers often appear to be _____.

- ☐ moving faster
- ☐ moving backward
- ☐ moving dangerously
- ☐ moving slower

Question 24 - Practice Test 3

At which locations should you always look both ways?

- ☐ Railroad crossings
- ☐ Crosswalks
- ☐ Intersections
- ☐ All of the above

Question 25 - Practice Test 3

When is it necessary to signal before passing another vehicle?

- ☐ Always
- ☐ Only if there are vehicles directly behind you
- ☐ If the driver of the vehicle may be unaware of your intention to pass
- ☐ On expressways with more than two lanes

Question 26 - Practice Test 3

When is it appropriate to use your horn?

- ☐ To warn pedestrians or other drivers of potential danger
- ☐ To encourage other drivers to drive faster
- ☐ To inform another driver of their mistake
- ☐ To tell pedestrians to get off the road

Question 27 - Practice Test 3

Which factor does not influence your blood alcohol concentration (BAC)?

- ☐ Time between drinks
- ☐ Your body weight
- ☐ Time since your last drink
- ☐ Type of alcohol consumed

Question 28 - Practice Test 3

Who is responsible for ensuring a child in the vehicle you're driving is properly restrained?

- ☐ The vehicle owner
- ☐ The child
- ☐ Yourself
- ☐ The child's parents

Question 29 - Practice Test 3

If a driver's left arm is extended out the window and bent upward, this indicates they intend to _____.

- ☐ proceed straight
- ☐ slow down or stop
- ☐ turn right
- ☐ turn left

Question 30 - Practice Test 3

A flashing red light signifies _____.

- ☐ caution
- ☐ slowing down
- ☐ the same as a stop sign
- ☐ the same as a yield sign

Question 31 - Practice Test 3

Which areas are most likely to ice over first in freezing temperatures?

- ☐ Bridges and overpasses
- ☐ Residential streets
- ☐ Tunnels
- ☐ Gravel roads

Question 32 - Practice Test 3

When a vehicle merges onto an expressway, who has the right-of-way?

- ☐ The merging vehicle
- ☐ The fastest vehicle
- ☐ Vehicles already on the expressway
- ☐ The slowest vehicle

Question 33 - Practice Test 3

You are the third vehicle to arrive at a four-way stop at different times. Which vehicle has the right-of-way?

- ☐ The vehicle that is not signaling
- ☐ The vehicle turning right
- ☐ The vehicle that arrived first
- ☐ The vehicle to your right

Question 34 - Practice Test 3

You approach a crosswalk with a pedestrian and guide dog attempting to cross the street. What should you do?

- ☐ Tell the pedestrian it is safe to cross
- ☐ Stop and turn off your engine
- ☐ Wait for the pedestrian to cross the street
- ☐ Honk your horn to indicate it is safe to cross

Question 35 - Practice Test 3

When can you safely merge back in front of a vehicle you just passed?

- ☐ When the driver honks to let you in
- ☐ When you see the entire front bumper of the passed vehicle in your rear-view mirror
- ☐ When you make direct eye contact with the driver in your rearview mirror.
- ☐ When you can't see the passing vehicle from the window.

Question 36 - Practice Test 3

If you're at a traffic light and a car is speeding toward you from behind, what should you do?

- ☐ Pull your vehicle forward
- ☐ Execute a quick U-turn
- ☐ Maneuver your vehicle to the left
- ☐ Maneuver your vehicle to the right

Question 37 - Practice Test 3

What are the main aids for a blind person when traveling?

- ☐ A red cane or a trained guide cat
- ☐ A white cane or a wheelchair
- ☐ A red cane or a trained guide dog
- ☐ A white cane or a trained guide dog

Question 38 - Practice Test 3

The distance your vehicle covers from the time you recognize a hazard until you begin to brake is known as _____.

- ☐ the perception distance
- ☐ the stopping distance
- ☐ the reaction distance
- ☐ the braking distance

Question 39 - Practice Test 3

When you're at a railroad crossing that's marked only with a stop sign, when is it safe to proceed?

- ☐ When no train appears to be coming
- ☐ When no pedestrians are coming
- ☐ When no school children are around
- ☐ All of the above

The state of drowsiness or unawareness during freeway driving is known as highway hypnosis. How can you avoid it?

☐   By frequently shifting your gaze

☐   By listening to loud music

☐   By regularly talking on your cell phone

☐   By frequently changing lanes

INTERACTIVE ROAD SIGNS FLASHCARDS

Mastering road signs is a crucial part of your DMV exam preparation. Recognizing and understanding these signs not only helps you pass the test but also ensures you're a safer, more informed driver on the road. To help you solidify your knowledge of road signs, we've created an interactive online tool that you can access from anywhere.

Why Use Flashcards?

Flashcards are a proven study method that can significantly boost your memory retention. By repeatedly testing yourself on the meanings of various road signs, you can quickly identify areas where you need more practice and reinforce the information you already know. They are an effective way to review key concepts in a short amount of time, making them perfect for busy schedules.

Access Our Interactive Flashcards Online

We've developed an awesome online resource where you can practice with digital flashcards designed specifically for road signs. This tool is interactive, easy to use, and accessible from your computer, tablet, or smartphone. Whether you're at home, on your lunch break, or waiting in line, you can take a few minutes to review and test your knowledge.

Access the Flashcards Here:
expert-driving-school.webflow.io

You can also scan the QR code below with your mobile device to access the flashcards instantly:

How to Use the Flashcards

- **Daily Practice:** Set aside a few minutes each day to go through the flashcards. Consistent, short study sessions are more effective than cramming.
- **Test Yourself:** Go through the flashcards in random order to ensure you're not just memorizing the sequence.
- **Track Your Progress:** Note which signs you find challenging and revisit them until you're confident.
- **On-the-Go Learning:** The convenience of accessing these flashcards online means you can fit study sessions into your daily routine, whether you're commuting, on a break, or relaxing at home.

Making the Most of This Resource

The road to passing your DMV exam is made smoother with the right tools, and our interactive flashcards are designed to give you an edge. Combine this resource with the other study materials in this workbook to ensure you're thoroughly prepared.

Remember, understanding road signs is not just about passing the test—it's about becoming a responsible, informed driver. Use these flashcards to build that essential knowledge, and enjoy the confidence that comes with knowing you're ready for the road.

ROAD SIGNS

In the United States, the trend is moving towards using symbols instead of words on road signs for more effective communication. These symbols break down language barriers and facilitate immediate understanding, quickly becoming the global norm for traffic control devices.

It's imperative for all drivers to be well-versed with these traffic sign symbols to ensure the smooth functioning and safety of our transportation networks.

Don't worry, we've got your back. Our resource includes over 50 questions focused on Road Signs to help you master this vital aspect.

Total Questions: 50
Correct Answer to pass: 40

Question 1 - Road Signs

What does this image represent?

- ☐ When the way ahead is clear, passing on the left is permitted
- ☐ Passing on the right is not permitted
- ☐ Passing is prohibited in both directions
- ☐ Passing is only permitted during night

Question 2 - Road Signs

What exactly does this road sign mean?

□   A construction zone is ahead

□   There is a parking area ahead

□   There is a forest zone is ahead

□   There's a rest stop ahead

Question 3 - Road Signs

What does this image represent?

□   A child care center

□   T-intersection ahead

□   Playground ahead

□   School zone ahead

Question 4 - Road Signs

What does this sign denote?

- ○   A side street near a railroad crossing

- ○   A bridge

- ○   A Truck service center

- ○   A pedestrian underpass

Question 5 - Road Signs

This symbol denotes

- ○   a hospital zone

- ○   wheelchair accessibility

- ○   a parking area for the handicapped

- ○   a pedestrian crosswalk

Question 6 - Road Signs

This orange triangular reflective sign indicates

☐　　a vehicle that moves in a rapid pace

☐　　a vehicle transporting hazardous materials

☐　　a vehicle that moves slowly

☐　　a truck

Question 7 - Road Signs

Which of these signs points you in the direction of a hospital?

A　B　C　D

☐　　C

☐　　B

☐　　A

☐　　D

Question 8 - Road Signs

What does this sign indicate?

☐   Do not accelerate to 45 mph

☐   Drive at a 45-mph speed

☐   There is a speed zone is ahead; prepare to slow down to 45 mph

☐   Construction zone ahead

Question 9 - Road Signs

Typically, a vertical rectangular traffic sign gives

☐   instructions to the driver

☐   directions to the driver to come to a halt

☐   a warning about the construction work

☐   a warning about the road's condition

Question 10 - Road Signs

This symbol denotes

☐   a lane for turning left

☐   a diversion

☐   that the road ahead curves to the left

☐   a lane for turning right

Question 11 - Road Signs

This symbol indicates

☐   railroad crossing

☐   road work

☐   a right turn

☐   road maintenance

Question 12 - Road Signs

What is the significance of this flashing arrow panel?

☐   The lane ahead of you has been closed

☐   The lane ahead is open for traffic

☐   Flaggers are in front

☐   There are right lane curves ahead

Question 13 - Road Signs

What does this sign indicate?

☐   A divided highway begins ahead

☐   One-way traffic ahead

☐   The divided highway ends ahead

☐   Merging Traffic

Question 14 - Road Signs

What is the meaning of this sign?

☐   When the green arrow is ON, left turns are permitted

☐   When the steady green signal is lit and there are no oncoming vehicles, left turns are permitted

☐   When the green arrow goes out, no left turns are permitted

☐   Left turns are only permitted when the steady green signal is OFF

Question 15 - Road Signs

What exactly does this sign mean?

☐   There is disabled parking ahead.

☐   There is a disabled crossing ahead.

☐   A hospital is on the way.

☐   There is a pedestrian crosswalk ahead.

Question 16 - Road Signs

This warning sign informs drivers that

☐   a single-use path crossing ahead

☐   there is a school zone ahead

☐   it is a bicycle lane

☐   a multi-use path crossing is ahead

Question 17 - Road Signs

This symbol indicates that

☐   bicyclists should only ride in the lane designated by the sign

☐   there is a bikeway crosses the road ahead

☐   bicyclists are not allowed to use this lane

☐   there is a no-passing zone for bicyclists ahead

Question 18 - Road Signs

If you see this sign while driving in the left lane, what should you do?

- ☐ continue straight
- ☐ merge into the right lane
- ☐ turn left
- ☐ turn right

Question 19 - Road Signs

This warning sign indicates

- ☐ there will be sharp right and left turns
- ☐ the road ahead takes a left turn
- ☐ a winding road
- ☐ that the road ahead bends to the right, then to the left

Question 20 - Road Signs

What does this signal indicate at an intersection?

- ☐ Pedestrians are not allowed to enter the crosswalk
- ☐ Drivers must slow down
- ☐ Pedestrians who are already in the crosswalk may finish their crossing
- ☐ Pedestrians are permitted to enter the crosswalk

Question 21 - Road Signs

What does this symbol indicate?

- ☐ A hospital ahead
- ☐ There is a rest stop ahead
- ☐ High school ahead
- ☐ Handicapped service

Question 22 - Road Signs

This symbol indicates

- ☐   the exit number 117 is up ahead
- ☐   next available exit is 117 miles away
- ☐   to enter the Route 117, take this exit
- ☐   none of the above

Question 23 - Road Signs

This sign indicates the location of

- ☐   a gas station
- ☐   a handicapped service
- ☐   a rest zone
- ☐   a hospital zone

Question 24 - Road Signs

What does this sign mean?

☐   Speed limit ahead

☐   Speed restriction on-ramp

☐   Speed advisory at roundabout

☐   An exit speed restriction

Question 25 - Road Signs

What exactly does this sign mean?

☐   Only left turns are permitted

☐   Traffic must merge to the right

☐   Traffic must merge to the left

☐   Only right turns are permitted

Question 26 - Road Signs

What exactly does this sign mean?

    ☐   You shouldn't take a right turn

    ☐   You must not take a left turn

    ☐   This section of the road is closed

    ☐   Do not merge

Question 27 - Road Signs

What exactly does this sign mean?

    ☐   A hospital zone

    ☐   Telephone service available ahead

    ☐   Gas station ahead

    ☐   There will be a rest zone ahead

Question 28 - Road Signs

What exactly does this sign indicate?

   ☐   You are about to approach a left turn

   ☐   You are about to approach a right turn

   ☐   A sharp U-turn

   ☐   A sharp left turn ahead

Question 29 - Road Signs

What should you do if you see this road sign?

   ☐   Exit the highway at a speed of at least 30 miles per hour

   ☐   Exit the highway at a speed of no more than 30 miles per hour

   ☐   Increase your speed to 30 mph to pass the vehicle in front of you

   ☐   Exit the freeway at a top speed of 60 mph

Question 30 - Road Signs

This pavement markings in this image indicate that

- ☐ It is not allowed to pass

- ☐ You can pass if it is safe

- ☐ Take a detour

- ☐ Make a U turn

Question 31 - Road Signs

What is the meaning of this traffic sign?

- ☐ It is not permissible to pass a vehicle on the left

- ☐ Only left turns are allowed

- ☐ Passing is legal in these directions

- ☐ Only move in the indicated directions

Question 32 - Road Signs

What does this sign mean?

- ☐   Hospital Zone
- ☐   You are approaching a A four-way intersection
- ☐   A side road is ahead
- ☐   A railroad crossing is ahead

Question 33 - Road Signs

What does this symbol indicate?

- ☐   Railroad crossing with low ground clearance
- ☐   Railroad crossing that is closed
- ☐   Railroad crossing that is being repaired
- ☐   Byway near a railroad crossing

Question 34 - Road Signs

What does this image mean?

- ☐   A broken white line that forbids passing
- ☐   A broken white line that permits passing
- ☐   An accident occurred
- ☐   The vehicle is making a U-turn

Question 35 - Road Signs

This is an octagonal (eight-sided) figure which indicates

- ☐   a Yield symbol
- ☐   Do Not Enter sign
- ☐   a Stop sign
- ☐   a Construction sign

Question 36 - Road Signs

You can find this orange sign at

☐   railroad crossings

☐   the intersections that are uncontrolled

☐   school zones

☐   work zones

Question 37 - Road Signs

What does this sign indicate?

☐   A winding road

☐   A curve ahead

☐   A slippery road

☐   A two-way road

Question 38 - Road Signs

What does this sign denote?

- ☐ A winding road awaits; drivers should follow the signs
- ☐ A gravel road ahead with sharp curves; drivers must proceed with caution
- ☐ When the road is wet, it becomes slippery; proceed cautiously
- ☐ A sharp curve near a hill; vehicles must proceed cautiously

Question 39 - Road Signs

What does this sign indicate?

- ☐ "Right Lane Ends"
- ☐ Freeway interchange
- ☐ Sharp turn on a highway
- ☐ Beginning of a Divided Highway

Question 40 - Road Signs

What does this sign indicate?

○   You are not permitted to park on both sides of the sign

○   You can park on the left side of the sign

○   Parking is available to the right of the sign

○   You are not allowed to park to the left of the sign

Question 41 - Road Signs

What does this sign mean?

○   The divided highway ends

○   A divided highway begins ahead

○   There's an underpass ahead

○   Right lane is closed

Question 42 - Road Signs

This sign means that you are

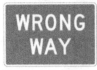

- ☐ in a wrong lane
- ☐ driving in the wrong direction
- ☐ In the city
- ☐ moving in a bicycle lane

Question 43 - Road Signs

What exactly does this sign mean?

- ☐ Take Route 45
- ☐ The top speed is 45 miles per hour any time
- ☐ The minimum speed limit is 45 miles per hour
- ☐ The maximum speed limit at night is 45 mph

Question 44 - Road Signs

What exactly does this sign indicate?

○   Emergency vehicles may enter the roadway

○   Trucks transporting dangerous materials may enter the road

○   Heavy vehicles may enter the road

○   Farm vehicles may enter the roadway

Question 45 - Road Signs

What should you do if you come across this sign at an intersection?

○   Do not move further

○   Continue right

○   Allow oncoming traffic to pass

○   Before turning right or left, yield the right-of-way or stop

Question 46 - Road Signs

What exactly does this sign indicate?

☐   At the sign, all vehicles must make a U-turn

☐   U-turns are not permitted for trucks

☐   Vehicles are not permitted to make a U-turn at the sign

☐   It denotes none of the preceding

Question 47 - Road Signs

What does this sign mean?

☐   A side road is ahead

☐   A T-intersection is ahead; yield to cross traffic

☐   A four-way stop ahead; prepare to yield

☐   A tourist information center is ahead

Question 48 - Road Signs

What exactly does this sign mean?

☐   A deer crossing ahead

☐   Cattle crossing ahead

☐   Forest zone

☐   A zoo ahead

Question 49 - Road Signs

What does this sign indicate?

☐   The maximum allowable speed in a school zone

☐   The minimum allowable speed in a school zone

☐   When there are children present in a school zone, this is the maximum allowable speed

☐   When there are children present in a school zone, this is the minimum allowable speed

What does this sign mean?

O   Parking available

O   Lodging available

O   Hospital service available

O   Handicapped service area available

SIGNS AND SITUATIONS

Presented here is a comprehensive assortment of Signs and Scenarios specifically designed to enhance your understanding of intersections and shared lanes. This collection is not just an assortment of random signs and situations but a carefully curated set of content meant to address all possible scenarios you may encounter on the road.

Total Questions: 25
Correct Answer to pass: 20

Question 1 - Signs & Situations

When you park your vehicle facing downhill next to a curb, in which direction should you turn your front wheels?

- ☐   Away from the curb

- ☐   Keep them straight

- ☐   Toward the curb

- ☐   It doesn't matter

Question 2 - Signs & Situations

You approach an intersection where the traffic lights are completely out. What should you do?

- ☐   Yield as you would at a yield sign

- ☐   Treat the intersection as if there are no signs or signals

- ☐   Treat the intersection like an all-way stop

- ☐   Proceed with caution

Question 3 - Signs & Situations

You notice a lane with white diamonds painted on it. What do they imply?

- ☐   This is a bus only lane
- ☐   This is a stop lane for emergencies
- ☐   This lane is now closed
- ☐   This is a reserved lane

Question 4 - Signs & Situations

At around the same moment, two cars arrive at an intersection. Which of the following statements is correct?

- ☐   All vehicles turning left must yield to Car B
- ☐   The drivers must select who will drive first
- ☐   Car A must yield since it is making a left turn
- ☐   None of the preceding statements are correct

Question 5 - Signs & Situations

You've parked facing a steep downhill slope. Which of the following actions should you take?

☐   If you have a manual transmission, keep it in reverse

☐   If you have a manual transmission, keep it in first gear

☐   If you have an automatic transmission, keep it in first gear

☐   If you have an automatic transmission, keep it in reverse

Question 6 - Signs & Situations

Three vehicles reach an intersection simultaneously. Who has the right-of-way?

☐   Vehicle B

☐   Vehicle A

☐   The pedestrian

☐   Vehicle C

You notice a yellow "X" light flashing above your lane. What does it imply?

☐   You should exit this lane as soon as possible

☐   This lane is now closed

☐   This lane is clear

☐   This lane is only for turning left

Question 8 - Signs & Situations

You have parked uphill on a steep incline. What should you do?

☐   Set your automatic transmission to first gear

☐   Set your automatic transmission to reverse

☐   Set your manual transmission to first gear

☐   Set your manual transmission to reverse

Question 9 - Signs & Situations

Which of the following takes priority (i.e., should be obeyed above all the others)?

- ☐ A red traffic light
- ☐ A traffic officer
- ☐ A stopped school bus with flashing red lights
- ☐ A warning road sign

Question 10 - Signs & Situations

What should you do when you see a flashing red light?

- ☐ You are not required to stop or yield at a flashing red signal
- ☐ Stop, yield, and then proceed when it is safe to do so
- ☐ Proceed with caution because the traffic signal is out
- ☐ Stop and hold your breath until the light turns green

Question 11 - Signs & Situations

What does the following sign indicate?

- ☐ The minimum speed for this curve is 35 mph
- ☐ The maximum speed for this curve is 35 mph
- ☐ The recommended speed for this curve is 35 mph
- ☐ The curve ahead is 35 degrees

Question 12 - Signs & Situations

You approach an intersection and notice this sign (red octagon shape). What are your options?

☐　　Stop completely and yield to traffic before proceeding

☐　　Stop completely and then proceed

☐　　Find another route; you cannot proceed through here

☐　　Slow down and only proceed if the intersection is clear

Question 13 - Signs & Situations

When can you drive in a lane with this sign?

☐　　When there is at least one passenger

☐　　Whenever you want

☐　　When at least two passengers are aboard

☐　　Never (this is a bus and truck lane)

Question 14 - Signs & Situations

At the same moment, two cars arrive at an uncontrolled intersection (one that is not controlled by signs or signals). Which of the following statements is correct?

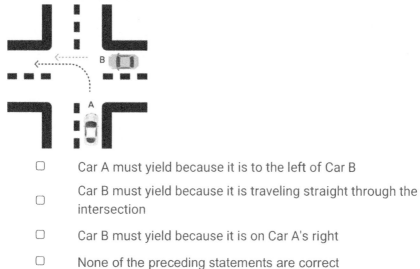

☐   Car A must yield because it is to the left of Car B

☐   Car B must yield because it is traveling straight through the intersection

☐   Car B must yield because it is on Car A's right

☐   None of the preceding statements are correct

Question 15 - Signs & Situations

You approach a crossroad with a green light and wish to drive straight through the intersection. Which of the following is correct?

☐   You are unable to proceed

☐   You are free to continue

☐   You may proceed, but you must first yield to any vehicles already present in the crossroads

☐   You must temporarily stop and cede before proceeding

Car B enters an intersection intending to turn right on a red light, while Car A has a green light and wants to proceed straight through the intersection. Which statement is accurate?

- ☐ Car A should yield to Car B
- ☐ Car A must accelerate to pass Car B
- ☐ Car B should stop and allow Car A to pass
- ☐ None of these options are correct

Question 17 - Signs & Situations

Before turning left into a driveway, to whom must you yield?

- ☐ Approaching vehicles
- ☐ Pedestrians
- ☐ Both pedestrians and oncoming vehicles
- ☐ No one (you have the right-of-way)

Question 18 - Signs & Situations

Which of the following is correct about driving in rainy conditions?

- ☐ Roads tend to be most slippery during the first 30 minutes of rain
- ☐ Avoid using cruise control when driving on wet roads
- ☐ Turn on your headlights to improve visibility
- ☐ All of the above

Question 19 - Signs & Situations

You approach an intersection with a STOP sign. Where are you required to stop?

- ☐ Before entering the intersection
- ☐ In front of the stop line
- ☐ Prior to the crosswalk
- ☐ All of the above options apply

Question 20 - Signs & Situations

You arrive at a crossroads wanting to turn left with a green light. Can you proceed?

- ☐ Sure, but only if a Left Turn Permitted sign is present
- ☐ Sure, but first yield to pedestrians and oncoming traffic
- ☐ No, you may only turn left on a green arrow
- ☐ Sure, this is a "protected" turn, and you have the right-of-way

Question 21 - Signs & Situations

You have parked uphill next to a curb. In which direction should you point your front wheels?

☐ Away from the curb

☐ In any direction

☐ Towards the curb

☐ Straight

Question 22 - Signs & Situations

You approach an intersection and see the following red sign. What should you do?

☐ Slow down and be ready to yield to pedestrians and oncoming traffic

☐ Continue at your current speed since the traffic ahead must yield to you

☐ Slow down and prepare to yield to traffic ahead, but stopping is not necessary

☐ Come to a complete stop, yield to pedestrians and oncoming traffic, and then proceed

Question 23 - Signs & Situations

The driver is using a hand signal. He/She intends to:

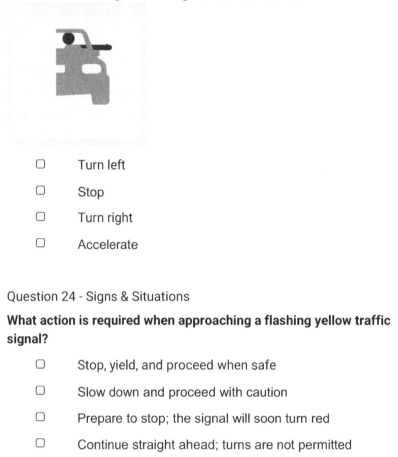

- ☐ Turn left
- ☐ Stop
- ☐ Turn right
- ☐ Accelerate

Question 24 - Signs & Situations

What action is required when approaching a flashing yellow traffic signal?

- ☐ Stop, yield, and proceed when safe
- ☐ Slow down and proceed with caution
- ☐ Prepare to stop; the signal will soon turn red
- ☐ Continue straight ahead; turns are not permitted

What is the appropriate hand signal to signify that you are slowing or stopping?

☐   Left arm extended straight out to the left

☐   Left arm making a circular motion

☐   Left arm pointing downward

☐   Left arm bent upwards

FINES & LIMITS

This particular segment is tailored to the laws of your State, featuring questions focused on Fines and Limits. It is known to be one of the most challenging sections, often being the stumbling block for many test-takers.

Total Questions: 10
Correct Answer to pass: 8

Question 1 - Fines & Limits

What are the potential consequences in Illinois if you don't maintain the legally mandated auto insurance coverage?

☐　　License suspension

☐　　You'll be fined

☐　　Suspension of your vehicle's registration

☐　　All of the mentioned consequences will occur

Question 2 - Fines & Limits

When you're driving on a roadway in Illinois, what are you implicitly consenting to?

☐　　Your residence being searched

☐　　Your medical records being examined

☐　　Undergoing blood, breath, or urine tests

☐　　All of the above

Question 3 - Fines & Limits

What does an Illinois Occupational Driving Permit (ODP) grant a professional driver whose license has been suspended due to three moving violations?

- ☐ Driving to and from social events
- ☐ Driving for medical reasons
- ☐ Driving as part of their job
- ☐ Driving to and from school

Question 4 - Fines & Limits

In Illinois, how many moving violations within a span of two years will lead to at least a 30-day license suspension for a driver under 21?

- ☐ 4 or more
- ☐ 2 or more
- ☐ 3 or more
- ☐ 1 or more

Question 5 - Fines & Limits

After a DUI arrest in Illinois, the officer seizes your driver's license and issues you a temporary receipt. How long does this receipt allow you to continue driving until the suspension period commences?

- ☐ 4 months
- ☐ 45 days
- ☐ 5 months
- ☐ 5 days

Illinois law prohibits alcohol consumption in vehicles for most residents. Who are NOT subject to this prohibition?

☐ Passengers in chartered buses

☐ Limousine passengers

☐ Passengers in motor homes

☐ Automobile backseat passengers

Before applying for a standard driver's license, how long must a 16-year-old driver hold a valid instruction permit in Illinois?

☐ 9 months

☐ 6 months

☐ 30 days

☐ 1 year

If a driver is caught driving with a Blood Alcohol Concentration (BAC) of 0.08% or higher in Illinois, what is the minimum duration for which their license will be suspended?

☐ 1 year

☐ 30 days

☐ 90 days

☐ 6 months

Question 9 - Fines & Limits

If a driver under the age of 21 in Illinois is given court supervision for an alcohol-related offense, how long will their driver's license be suspended?

☐   6 months

☐   1 month

☐   3 months

☐   2 months

Question 10 - Fines & Limits

Who does the Illinois safety belt law mandate to wear seat belts?

☐   The driver and front seat passengers

☐   Only the driver

☐   The driver and back seat passengers

☐   Everyone in the vehicle who is 8 years or older

DISTRACTED DRIVING TEST

This section is of paramount importance. It will probe your understanding of contemporary driving distractions, along with the implications of driving under the influence of drugs and medication.

Total Questions: 18
Correct Answer to pass: 15

Question 1 - Distracted Driving

Which of the following statements about cell phones is accurate?

☐ It is quicker to make a call while driving

☐ The use of a hands-free cell phone while driving is permitted for adults

☐ Cell phones can be used while driving for adults

☐ If you get a call while you're driving, you should slow down before answering

Question 2 - Distracted Driving

Something happening in the backseat requires your attention while you are driving. What should you do?

☐ As you continue to drive, slow down and handle the issue

☐ Turn around and cope with the situation, occasionally looking ahead

☐ Before addressing the issue, pull over to the side of the road and park your vehicle

☐ You should adjust the rearview mirror to see the back seat

Question 3 - Distracted Driving

What should you do before driving if you feel sleepy?

- ☐ Sleep
- ☐ Music-listening
- ☐ consume coffee
- ☐ Exercise

Question 4 - Distracted Driving

What medications, excluding alcohol, can impair one's capacity for safe driving?

- ☐ Prescription drugs
- ☐ Non-prescription medications
- ☐ Medications used to treat migraines, colds, hay fever, various allergies, or to soothe the nerves
- ☐ The entire list above

Question 5 - Distracted Driving

Is it safe to take medications before driving?

- ☐ Only with a valid prescription
- ☐ No
- ☐ Only if the physician states that it won't impair safe driving
- ☐ Only over-the-counter versions

Question 6 - Distracted Driving

It's _____ to text and drive.

- ☐ legal
- ☐ legal if you do not exceed 15 mph
- ☐ legal only when you stop at a STOP sign
- ☐ illegal

Question 7 - Distracted Driving

Talking on a cell phone while driving increases the likelihood of a collision _____.

- ☐ up to four times
- ☐ up to three times
- ☐ by some more amount
- ☐ at least twice

Question 8 - Distracted Driving

Is it legal for teenage drivers to talk on their cell phones while driving?

- ☐ Only when traveling at less than 25 mph
- ☐ Only if you're on a country road
- ☐ Yes, as long as you're cautious
- ☐ It is illegal to use a cell phone while driving

Question 9 - Distracted Driving

To avoid being a distracted driver, you should:

☐ smoke, eat, and drink only on straight sections of the road

☐ consult maps or use your phone when no other vehicles are around you

☐ have all emotionally challenging conversations during your initial hour of driving

☐ If possible, switch off your cell phone until you arrive at your destination

Question 10 - Distracted Driving

Fatigue can impact your driving by

☐ Compromising your judgment

☐ Slowing down your reaction times

☐ Reducing your awareness

☐ All of the above

Question 11 - Distracted Driving

Potential distractions while driving include:

☐ Constantly checking mirrors

☐ Checking blind spots

☐ Frequently checking the traffic behind you

☐ Text messaging and talking on the phone

Question 12 - Distracted Driving

Is it safe to hold something in your lap while driving?

- ☐ Yes, as long as it's not a human or a pet
- ☐ Yes, if it's a small animal
- ☐ Yes, as long as you don't get distracted
- ☐ No way, never

Question 13 - Distracted Driving

To combat highway hypnosis, drowsiness, and fatigue, drivers should _____ to stay awake while driving.

- ☐ Take stimulants
- ☐ Do exercise with their eyes
- ☐ Text message their loved ones
- ☐ Talk on a cell phone

Question 14 - Distracted Driving

Which of the following activities will not negatively affect your driving on the road?

- ☐ Eating
- ☐ Smoking
- ☐ Drinking coffee
- ☐ Listening to the radio

Question 15 - Distracted Driving

A minor driver receives a phone call on their cell phone. He/she should:

- ☐ not carry a cell phone while driving
- ☐ not answer the call
- ☐ use a hands-free cell phone to answer the call
- ☐ answer the call only in an emergency

Question 16 - Distracted Driving

Which of the following actions will NOT help prevent distracted driving?

- ☐ Preprogramming your favorite radio stations
- ☐ Adjusting all your mirrors before starting
- ☐ Pre-loosening the coffee cup lid
- ☐ Preplanning the route

Question 17 - Distracted Driving

Which of the following actions is NOT a safe driving practice?

- ☐ Texting and operating visual screen devices while driving
- ☐ Looking forward and sideways while parking
- ☐ Using side mirrors while you drive
- ☐ Humming to music while you drive

Question 18 - Distracted Driving

Be aware of the following potential distractions or impairments while driving:

☐   Alcohol, drugs, and certain medications

☐   Adjusting electronic controls and vehicle features

☐   Listening to loud music, using devices such as cell phones, GPS, and intercoms

☐   All of the above mentioned

DRINKING AND DRIVING TEST

This segment delves into the repercussions of driving under the influence of alcohol. It's essential to grasp the restrictions associated with alcohol consumption and its impact on your physical condition while driving.

Total Questions: 20
Correct Answer to pass: 16

Question 1 - Drinking and Driving

If you're unable to drive due to excessive alcohol consumption, what should you do?

- ☐ Have a designated driver take you home
- ☐ Call 911 for assistance in driving
- ☐ Drink coffee to stay awake while driving
- ☐ Take drugs to counteract the effects of alcohol before driving

Question 2 - Drinking and Driving

What can help an intoxicated person sober up?

- ☐ Time
- ☐ A cup of coffee
- ☐ Cold and fresh air
- ☐ All of the above

Question 3 - Drinking and Driving

What are the potential penalties for being convicted of driving under the influence of alcohol or drugs?

☐ License suspension

☐ Substantial fines and higher insurance rates

☐ Community service

☐ Any or all of the above

Question 4 - Drinking and Driving

Which is NOT a consequence of consuming alcohol?

☐ Increased alertness

☐ Slow reactions

☐ Impaired judgment

☐ Hindered vision

Question 5 - Drinking and Driving

Which of the following beverages has a standard 1.5-ounce amount of alcohol?

☐ A 5-ounce glass of wine

☐ One can of beer

☐ One shot of 80-proof liquor

☐ Each of the above

Question 6 - Drinking and Driving

Why is consuming alcohol and driving at night particularly dangerous?

- ☐ Alcohol impairs judgment more at night
- ☐ There's a higher chance of encountering drunk drivers
- ☐ Vision is already restricted
- ☐ Roads are busier at night

Question 7 - Drinking and Driving

Which factor does not impact blood alcohol concentration?

- ☐ Time during which alcohol was consumed
- ☐ Body weight
- ☐ Time since the last drink
- ☐ Alcohol type

Question 8 - Drinking and Driving

How does alcohol consumption impact driving ability?

- ☐ Reduces driving skills
- ☐ Negatively affects depth perception
- ☐ Slows down reflexes
- ☐ All of the above

Question 9 - Drinking and Driving

Which of the following actions will result in the mandatory suspension of a minor's license?

- ☐ Driving when impaired by drugs
- ☐ Transporting an open beer container
- ☐ Transporting an open liquor container
- ☐ Any or all of the preceding

Question 10 - Drinking and Driving

What is the leading cause of death for Americans aged 16 to 24?

- ☐ Kidney problems
- ☐ Drunk driving
- ☐ Drug overdose
- ☐ Cancer

Question 11 - Drinking and Driving

It is prohibited to have open containers of alcohol in a vehicle in which of the following places?

- ☐ The driver's seat
- ☐ The console
- ☐ beneath the seat
- ☐ In all of the preceding

Question 12 - Drinking and Driving

Alcohol can have an impact on your:

- ☐ Reaction time
- ☐ Judgment
- ☐ Concentration
- ☐ All of the answers given above are correct.

Question 13 - Drinking and Driving

Drinking and driving can _____.

- ☐ Impair your reflexes
- ☐ Reduce physical control over a vehicle
- ☐ Decrease a driver's awareness of road hazards
- ☐ All of the above

Question 14 - Drinking and Driving

Which of the following statements about drivers under the age of twenty-one is correct?

- ☐ They are not permitted to purchase, drink, or possess alcohol
- ☐ They are permitted to consume limited amounts of alcohol, but not while driving
- ☐ They can buy alcohol but not consume it. They can have trace levels of alcohol in their blood while driving
- ☐ They are allowed to have trace amounts of alcohol in their blood while driving

Question 15 - Drinking and Driving

After consuming a significant amount of alcohol, you can ensure you will not be driving under the influence by:

- ☐ Waiting a day or two
- ☐ Drinking only beer or wine, not hard liquor
- ☐ Waiting at least an hour
- ☐ Waiting at least 30 minutes

Question 16 - Drinking and Driving

Which of the following regions does NOT allow open containers of alcohol?

- ☐ Passenger areas of standard passenger cars
- ☐ Limousine passenger compartments
- ☐ In a passenger car's trunk
- ☐ Motorhome residential areas

Question 17 - Drinking and Driving

Which of the following is an acceptable substitute for drinking and driving?

- ☐ Public transportation
- ☐ A designated driver
- ☐ A taxi
- ☐ All of the preceding

Question 18 - Drinking and Driving

A driver who has consumed alcohol is more likely to _____.

- ☐ fail to dim headlights for oncoming traffic
- ☐ drive too fast or too slowly
- ☐ change lanes frequently
- ☐ do all of the preceding tasks

Question 19 - Drinking and Driving

As a driver's blood alcohol concentration (BAC) increases, which of the following occurs?

- ☐ Alcohol impairs coordination and muscle control
- ☐ Alcohol has a growing impact on the brain of the drinker
- ☐ The first processes to be impacted are self-control and judgment
- ☐ All of the aforementioned

Question 20 - Drinking and Driving

How many standard servings of alcohol can an adult safely consume before driving?

- ☐ It varies depending on the individual.
- ☐ 2
- ☐ 1
- ☐ 3

MOCK TEST

This is the final part of the book. Sit back, relax, and focus. This practice test contains the same number of questions as the official DMV exam. Good luck! If you find yourself still making too many mistakes, we strongly recommend downloading the additional 200 questions in the resource section to further prepare for the exam!

Total Questions: 35
Correct Answer to pass: 28

Question 1 - Mock Exam

The two types of speed signs are:

- ☐ Informational speed signs and advisory speed signs
- ☐ Accident speed signs and advisory speed signs
- ☐ Speed limit signs and advisory speed signs
- ☐ Accident speed signs and regulatory speed signs

Question 2 - Mock Exam

If there are no warning devices or only a crossbuck sign at a railroad crossing, you should:

- ☐ Decrease your speed and proceed with caution
- ☐ Change gears and continue across the railroad crossing
- ☐ Stop within 100 feet of the railroad crossing
- ☐ Speed up and cross the railroad crossing

Question 3 - Mock Exam

When another vehicle from a different road is merging onto the road you are on, you must:

○ Use your horn to alert the merging traffic of your presence

○ Disregard the merging traffic since you have the right of way

○ Adjust your speed and vehicle position to accommodate the merging traffic

○ Change lanes immediately

Question 4 - Mock Exam

You must legally maintain a minimum safe distance of _____ when overtaking a bicycle moving in the same direction.

○ 5 feet

○ 10 feet

○ 7 feet

○ 3 feet

Question 5 - Mock Exam

Which statement about railroad crossings is incorrect?

○ Before crossing, you should verify the number of tracks

○ It's wise to change gears when crossing railroad tracks

○ You must yield to trains crossing

○ You should never begin crossing if your vehicle won't fit on the other side

Which statement about highway interchanges is incorrect?

- ☐ If you accidentally exit at the wrong interchange, you must follow it out
- ☐ The two most typical types of interchanges are diamond and cloverleaf
- ☐ If you miss your interchange, proceed to the next one
- ☐ If you miss your interchange, use a median crossover to turn around

Question 7 - Mock Exam

To prevent sudden braking or the need to turn abruptly, you should ____ while driving in the city.

- ☐ employ the one-second rule
- ☐ look two seconds ahead on the road
- ☐ adhere to the three-second rule
- ☐ look ten seconds ahead on the road

Question 8 - Mock Exam

A _____ demarcates the outer edge of a roadway, and can only be crossed by traffic moving to or from the shoulder.

- ☐ solid white line
- ☐ solid yellow line
- ☐ dashed white line
- ☐ dashed yellow line

Question 9 - Mock Exam

When approaching a STOP sign, you must _____.

- ☐ stop at the solid white stop line
- ☐ stop at the dashed white stop line
- ☐ stop at the edge of the road
- ☐ stop at the dashed yellow stop line

Question 10 - Mock Exam

If you are in an intersection and hear the siren of an emergency vehicle, what should you do?

- ☐ Stop in the intersection and move over to the right
- ☐ Continue through the intersection, then move over to the right and stop
- ☐ Stop in the intersection and move over to the left
- ☐ Continue through the intersection, then move over to the left and stop

Question 11 - Mock Exam

What type of lines signify pedestrian walkways?

- ☐ Crosswalk lines
- ☐ Pavement markings
- ☐ Stop lines
- ☐ Walking lines

Question 12 - Mock Exam

What should you do when driving downhill on a steep gradient?

☐ Press the gas pedal hard

☐ Shift into a lower gear

☐ Unfasten your seatbelt

☐ Turn on your headlights

Question 13 - Mock Exam

How should you react when a vehicle overtakes you from the left?

☐ Shift to the left lane

☐ Speed up to follow the vehicle

☐ Maintain your current speed

☐ Move to the right edge of the road

Question 14 - Mock Exam

What should you do if you're at a green light intersection and a pedestrian begins to cross against a red signal?

☐ Confront the pedestrian

☐ Allow the pedestrian to cross

☐ Stop and let the pedestrian cross

☐ Honk your horn to alert the pedestrian

Question 15 - Mock Exam

What speed should you maintain at a work zone when no reduced speed limits are posted?

☐   Follow the normal speed limit

☐   Drive over 70 mph

☐   Drive under 50 mph

☐   Maintain 45 mph

Question 16 - Mock Exam

When initiating a left turn from a two-way street onto a one-way street, where should you position your vehicle?

☐   Begin your turn with your right wheel as close as possible to the yellow dividing line

☐   Make a wide left turn

☐   Begin your turn with your left wheel as close as possible to the yellow dividing line

☐   Any of the above

Question 17 - Mock Exam

What should you avoid doing before making a right turn?

☐   Swing wide to the left

☐   Check your mirrors

☐   Signal your turn

☐   Wear your seat belt

Question 18 - Mock Exam

What type of lane is usually found at the end of freeway on-ramps, allowing for speed increase?

☐ Deceleration lane

☐ Acceleration lane

☐ Access ramp

☐ Slow lane

Question 19 - Mock Exam

What should you do before changing lanes?

☐ Check your side mirrors and rear-view mirror

☐ Look over your shoulder toward the rear and check your mirrors

☐ Look behind you and check your side mirrors

☐ Check your speed and look over your shoulder toward the rear

Question 20 - Mock Exam

When overtaking a large vehicle, at what point is it safe to merge back into the lane?

☐ When you can see its headlights in your rear-view mirror

☐ When you can see its headlights in your right-side mirror

☐ When you can see its headlights in your left side mirror

☐ When you can see its driver in your left side mirror

Question 21 - Mock Exam

What's incorrect about these statements?

- ☐ You should increase your following distance when bicycles are on the road
- ☐ Bicycles and motorcycles move and stop more slowly than anticipated
- ☐ Motorcycles have the right to the full width of a lane, just like other vehicles
- ☐ Sharing a lane with a motorcycle is never a good idea

Question 22 - Mock Exam

Adverse weather conditions such as rain, snow, or ice can affect your visibility and stopping distance. What should you do to ensure your vehicle can stop safely in these situations?

- ☐ Accelerate
- ☐ Frequently change lanes
- ☐ Increase your following distance
- ☐ Use high-beam headlights

Question 23 - Mock Exam

What's the correct procedure when you're behind another vehicle at night?

- ☐ Turn off your headlights
- ☐ Switch to high-beam headlights
- ☐ Dim your high-beam headlights
- ☐ Follow the vehicle closely

Question 24 - Mock Exam

What should you do when you approach an intersection intending to turn right?

- ☐   Stay as close to the right as possible
- ☐   Stay in the middle lane
- ☐   Stay on the shoulder
- ☐   Stay as close to the left as possible

Question 25 - Mock Exam

When joining a highway from an on-ramp, it's necessary to _____ in order to blend with the flow of traffic.

- ☐   speed up
- ☐   change lanes while speeding up
- ☐   suddenly drop your speed
- ☐   gradually decrease your speed

Question 26 - Mock Exam

The most critical control mechanism to use when skidding is _____.

- ☐   the headlights
- ☐   the gas pedal
- ☐   the anti-lock braking system (ABS)
- ☐   the steering wheel

Question 27 - Mock Exam

In areas with four or more lanes of traffic traveling in opposing directions, what do double solid yellow lines signify?

   ☐   The individual lanes of travel

   ☐   The center of the roadway

   ☐   The edge of the road

   ☐   None of the above

Question 28 - Mock Exam

When parking on a roadway is necessary, you should position your vehicle _____.

   ☐   as distant from the yellow line as possible

   ☐   as far from the curb as possible

   ☐   as far from traffic as possible

   ☐   as close to the center of the road as possible

Question 29 - Mock Exam

When should you activate your high-beam headlights?

   ☐   When driving on unfamiliar roads

   ☐   When driving in construction zones

   ☐   In areas where there might be people along the side of the road

   ☐   In all of the above scenarios

In a multilane highway, when are you allowed to drive on the left half?

- ☐ When avoiding an obstacle
- ☐ When overtaking another vehicle
- ☐ When making a left turn
- ☐ In any of the above scenarios

Question 31 - Mock Exam

When entering or exiting a roundabout, you should always _____.

- ☐ accelerate
- ☐ change lanes
- ☐ keep to the left
- ☐ stay to the right

Question 32 - Mock Exam

If you cannot perform a U-turn, what should you consider?

- ☐ A four-point turn
- ☐ A two-point turn
- ☐ A three-point turn
- ☐ A five-point turn

Question 33 - Mock Exam

Which of these statements about U-turns is incorrect?

- ☐ Always perform a U-turn at a location marked with a "No U-Turn" sign

- ☐ Do not perform a U-turn on a bend or near the top of a hill

- ☐ A U-turn should only be executed when it is safe

- ☐ Certain cities and towns prohibit U-turns

Question 34 - Mock Exam

You must stop your vehicle in all of the following circumstances, except when _____.

- ☐ encountering a flashing yellow traffic signal

- ☐ encountering a flashing red traffic signal

- ☐ confronted with a STOP sign

- ☐ facing a steady red traffic signal

Question 35 - Mock Exam

When leaving a high-speed, two-lane roadway, you should _____ if vehicles are following you.

- ☐ not decelerate suddenly

- ☐ apply the brakes hard

- ☐ slow down as soon as possible

- ☐ increase your speed

A MESSAGE FROM THE DRIVING SCHOOL

As we wrap up this workbook, we just wanted to say a big thank you! We're so glad you chose us to be a part of your journey towards mastering the art of driving. It's been an absolute pleasure helping you get closer to acing that DMV exam.

We genuinely care about your success and satisfaction, and we're always looking for ways to make our resources better. That's where you come in - we'd love to hear your thoughts about this workbook.

Your feedback is like gold dust to us. It not only helps us improve, but it also guides future learners who are just starting out on their driving journey. So, if you have a spare moment and liked this book, would you mind sharing your experience with this workbook?

Leaving a review is easy as pie. Just head over to where you bought the book and let us know what you think. For the paperback version, you can find a QR code on the back cover that will take you directly to the review page. Every single word you share matters to us, and we're really excited to hear about your learning journey. If you have found any issue or you have suggestions on how to improve this book, feel free to write to us at info@infiniteinkpress.org.

Once again, a big thank you for picking our workbook. We're cheering you on and wishing you all the best as you hit the road and put all that learning into action. Safe driving and take care!

Thank you so much,

Expert Driving School

ANSWER SHEET

PRACTICE TEST 1

Question 1 - Practice Test 1

(A) If you're joining a main road from a private road, driveway, or alley, it is necessary to completely stop your vehicle and give way to pedestrians and other road users.

Question 2 - Practice Test 1

(B) If traffic signals are non-functional, consider the intersection as an all-stop intersection. Stop fully, give way, and carefully proceed when it is safe.

Question 3 - Practice Test 1

(B) When changing lanes, attempting to overtake another vehicle, or merging into traffic, use your signal and assess for overtaking traffic by viewing your mirrors. Once the mirrors show it is safe to change lanes, verify your vehicle's blind spot by glancing over your shoulder to the rear in the direction of the lane change.

Question 4 - Practice Test 1

(C) When joining an interstate highway from an acceleration lane, you should match the speed of highway traffic, provided it doesn't require you to exceed the posted legal speed limit.

Question 5 - Practice Test 1

(C) On a one-way street with three or more traffic lanes, use the middle lanes for through travel and the exterior lanes for turning.

Question 6 - Practice Test 1

(A) It is unlawful to surpass the speed limit when overtaking. Ensure you have sufficient time and space to safely complete the overtaking maneuver.

Question 7 - Practice Test 1

(D) If another vehicle is overtaking you, maintain your position in your lane and do not speed up. Allow the other vehicle to safely overtake you.

Question 8 - Practice Test 1

(D) On a multilane road, a dashed white line separates two lanes of traffic moving in the same direction. Overtaking is permissible when it's safe.

Question 9 - Practice Test 1

(A) As a driver, you must yield to pedestrians when they are crossing within a marked or an unmarked crosswalk on your side of the roadway, especially if there are no traffic control signals.

Question 10 - Practice Test 1

(D) Diagonal yellow stripes on roads and highways suggest an upcoming road obstruction or a narrowing roadway.

Question 11 - Practice Test 1

(D) Should you need to refer to a map or directions, ensure that you pull over safely to the side of the road before reading.

Question 12 - Practice Test 1

(B) When driving in the open countryside with no nearby vehicles, it's appropriate to use your high-beam headlights. Even so, with high beams on, it's safer to drive at a slower speed than you would during the daytime.

Question 13 - Practice Test 1

(A) If visibility approaches zero due to heavy fog, safely pull off the road as much as you can and stop.

Question 14 - Practice Test 1

(D) Exhibiting road rage may involve actions like cutting off other vehicles, excessive honking, forcing another vehicle off the road, or tailgating.

Question 15 - Practice Test 1

(A) In scenarios where you're about to overtake a bicycle and a vehicle is approaching from the opposite direction, it's advisable to slow down, let the oncoming vehicle pass first, and then provide ample space for the bicycle as you overtake.

Question 16 - Practice Test 1

(B) A steady yellow arrow in the direction of left at an intersection is an indication that the signal is about to switch to red. If you're nearing the intersection, stop if you can do so safely.

Question 17 - Practice Test 1

(B) It's unsafe to make a U-turn on a curve or near the top of a hill if you're invisible to drivers coming from both directions. Moreover, U-turns should not be made where signs prohibit them.

Question 18 - Practice Test 1

(B) Maintaining alertness allows you to anticipate when you will need to stop. Sudden stopping is hazardous and typically a sign of a distracted driver. Braking abruptly might lead to skidding and loss of vehicle control. Plus, it can make it difficult for the drivers behind you to stop without rear-ending your vehicle. Try to spot hazards early to avoid panic stops.

Question 19 - Practice Test 1

(D) The vision test for getting a driver's license assesses 1) visual clarity: the sharpness of your vision; 2) peripheral vision: the breadth of your field of view while looking straight ahead; 3) color and depth perception.

Question 20 - Practice Test 1

(B) The monotony of expressway driving can lead to highway hypnosis, a state of drowsiness or unawareness. To prevent this, try to constantly shift your eyes around different parts of the roadway and focus on various objects both near and far, left and right.

Question 21 - Practice Test 1

(C) When navigating a corner, employ the hand-over-hand technique to turn the steering wheel. Don't use just one hand, as this may result in loss of control. Once the turn is completed, manually straighten the steering wheel. It could be hazardous to let it slide through your fingers.

Question 22 - Practice Test 1

(D) Pedestrians who are using a white cane or a guide dog are usually blind or visually impaired. Exercise extreme caution, as they may not be able to see you.

Question 23 - Practice Test 1

(A) If you see a Do Not Enter sign, it means you're trying to enter a one-way street, or another road you're not allowed on, in the wrong direction. This sign is also posted at expressway entrance ramps if you're going in the wrong way.

Question 24 - Practice Test 1

(B) In case of brake failure, use the brake pedal and pump it. This might temporarily restore enough brake fluid pressure to decelerate or halt your vehicle. Shift down to a lower gear, utilizing the engine's braking power to slow down your vehicle. Apply the parking or emergency brake slowly but be ready to release it if skidding begins. If all else fails, release the gas pedal, aim for open space or a mild slope, and let the vehicle slow down naturally. Avoid colliding with anything, particularly in a head-on manner.

Question 25 - Practice Test 1

(A) Passing on the shoulder is never allowed.

Question 26 - Practice Test 1

(A) Do not begin crossing railroad tracks unless you are certain you can cross without having to stop. Never change gears while crossing the tracks.

Question 27 - Practice Test 1

(C) A yellow traffic light is a warning indicating the signal is about to turn red. If you're already in the intersection, continue your left turn and clear the intersection safely.

Question 28 - Practice Test 1

(C) When overtaking, ensure you pass on the left at a safe distance. Only re-enter the original lane once you can see the entire front of the vehicle you've overtaken in your rear-view mirror. To return to the original lane, signal a right turn.

Question 29 - Practice Test 1

(D) Aggressive driving endangers people and property. If a driver behind you consistently flashes their headlights, avoid retaliation or confrontation with the driver. Instead, make way for them.

Question 30 - Practice Test 1

(C) If your vehicle begins to skid, stay calm, remove your foot from the gas pedal, and steer carefully in the direction of the skid. Refrain from braking, particularly if your vehicle does not have an anti-lock braking system (ABS). This method, known as "steering into the skid," will align the rear of your car with the front.

Question 31 - Practice Test 1

(B) The 'Zipper Merge' technique is a driving strategy that suggests a departure from the traditional practice of merging early upon seeing that a lane is about to end. Early merging often leads to extended traffic backups, an increase in accidents, and instances of road rage. This new approach suggests that on spotting the "lane closed ahead" sign and noticing traffic building up, you should remain in your current lane till you reach the merge point. From there, drivers should take turns to merge smoothly and safely into the continuing lane. In heavy, slow-moving traffic, it's safer to remain in your current lane till the merge point.

Question 32 - Practice Test 1

(D) You can legally park at the curb or edge of a public road. Be sure to park in such a way that you do not obstruct traffic and your parked car is clearly visible to vehicles coming from either direction.

Question 33 - Practice Test 1

(D) Parking within 15 feet of a fire hydrant is illegal.

Question 34 - Practice Test 1

(B) When encountering pedestrians on or crossing the road, you should slow down, yield, and prepare to stop.

Question 35 - Practice Test 1

(D) When stopped behind another vehicle on a hill, maintain a gap of about one car length. The car ahead may roll back when starting, and if you're too close, there could be a collision.

Question 36 - Practice Test 1

(B) A solid white line adjacent to your lane means you should stay in your lane unless a special situation calls for a lane change.

Question 37 - Practice Test 1

(B) Motorcycles, like other vehicles, require the full width of a lane for safe maneuvering. Never share a lane with a motorcycle, even if the lane is wide and the motorcyclist is riding off to one side.

Question 38 - Practice Test 1

(D) When you are making a left turn at an intersection, alley, or driveway, you need to give way to all traffic coming from the opposite direction.

Question 39 - Practice Test 1

(D) You should enter the freeway at a speed that's close to or matches the freeway traffic speed. Keep in mind that the legal speed limit on interstates is 70 mph. You should avoid stopping before merging into freeway traffic unless it's absolutely necessary. Vehicles already on the freeway have the right of way.

Question 40 - Practice Test 1

(C) When on a multi-lane roadway with multiple lanes in one direction, overtaking should be performed using the middle and left lanes.

PRACTICE TEST 2

Question 1 - Practice Test 2

(D) When heated, oil within the asphalt rises to the surface, and rainwater can further dislodge these oil deposits. This creates a more slippery surface until additional rainfall washes the oil away.

Question 2 - Practice Test 2

(B) When a vehicle's turn signals are not functioning, the driver must use hand and arm signals. A right turn is indicated by a 90-degree upward-pointing arm, a left turn is shown by an extended leftward arm, and slowing down or stopping is signaled by a 90-degree downward-pointing arm.

Question 3 - Practice Test 2

(D) If your engine stops working mid-curve, use both hands to firmly steer to the right side of the road. Losing engine power will mean losing power-assisted steering and brakes, necessitating more force on the steering wheel and brake pedal. Once stopped, shift to park (automatic transmission) or neutral (manual transmission) and attempt to restart the engine.

Question 4 - Practice Test 2

(C) Safety belts are known to save lives, including those in the rear seats. In an accident, they can significantly reduce the risk of serious injuries.

Question 5 - Practice Test 2

(B) Tailgating, or following too closely, is a primary reason for rear-end collisions on highways. It's crucial to keep a safe distance from the vehicle ahead.

Question 6 - Practice Test 2

(C) To prevent a head-on collision, steer right towards the shoulder or curb. Don't steer left; the other driver might attempt to correct their course. Be ready to entirely leave the roadway to the right if needed.

Question 7 - Practice Test 2

(C) Vehicles in a roundabout move around a central island in a counterclockwise direction. The design of these intersections is intended to reduce both the number and severity of collisions.

Question 8 - Practice Test 2

(D) When you're getting ready to leave a parallel parking spot, it's important to do all of the above. Check your mirrors, look over your shoulder, and signal your intention to move. Wait until the road is clear before pulling into traffic and stay in the nearest lane until it's safe to switch lanes.

Question 9 - Practice Test 2

(B) If your vehicle gets stuck on railroad tracks and a train is coming, avoid trying to free the vehicle. Instead, ensure everyone exits the vehicle and swiftly moves at a 45-degree angle away from the tracks in the direction the train is coming. This way, you and any passengers will not be hit by debris if the car is struck. Contact 911 or call the number displayed on the railroad crossing sign.

Question 10 - Practice Test 2

(A) When double solid lines are adjacent to your lane, passing or changing lanes is prohibited.

Question 11 - Practice Test 2

(D) When driving on wet pavement at speeds up to 35 mph, modern tires generally disperse water to maintain road contact. However, at higher speeds in deep water, tire channeling becomes less effective, causing the tires to glide on the water like water skis. This phenomenon is called "hydroplaning." At 50 mph or above, hydroplaning can lead to a complete loss of braking and steering control. To avoid hydroplaning, reduce your speed.

Question 12 - Practice Test 2

(C) When two vehicles meet on a steep mountain road where neither can pass, the vehicle descending must yield the right-of-way by reversing until the vehicle ascending can pass. The vehicle facing downhill has more control when backing up.

Question 13 - Practice Test 2

(C) You can avoid sudden, panic stops by identifying potential hazards well in advance and planning how to handle them. Abrupt stopping is dangerous and is usually indicative of a driver who is not paying attention. If you stop suddenly, you risk being rear-ended by the vehicle behind you or skidding and losing control of your vehicle.

Question 14 - Practice Test 2

(C) If your gas pedal is stuck, DON'T PANIC. Try to lift the gas pedal with your foot. If that doesn't work, switch your vehicle to neutral to disengage power to the drive wheels. Then, apply brakes to slow down and steer your vehicle off the road.

Question 15 - Practice Test 2

(B) Continually applying brakes to control your speed while descending a steep hill can cause brake fade, which reduces their effectiveness. Instead, release the gas pedal and shift into a lower gear (even with an automatic transmission). This will create a braking effect known as engine braking to slow down the vehicle. Apply brakes only when engine braking is insufficient or you want to stop. You should never coast downhill in neutral or (for manual transmissions) with the clutch depressed.

Question 16 - Practice Test 2

(C) On gravel or dirt roads, your vehicle doesn't have as much traction as on concrete or asphalt roads. This will extend your stopping distance, and you may skid when you turn. Therefore, slow down.

Question 17 - Practice Test 2

(C) If you're being tailgated, shift to the right lane and decrease your speed to encourage the tailgater to pass you on your left. Do not accelerate in an attempt to placate or outrun the tailgater. No speed is too fast for some tailgaters.

Question 18 - Practice Test 2

(D) Increasing your speed amplifies your braking distance as the square of the speed increases. If you double your speed, your braking distance becomes not twice as long but four times as long. If you triple your speed, your braking distance becomes nine times as long.

Question 19 - Practice Test 2

(A) Defensive driving, as defined by the National Safety Council, is "driving to save lives, time, and money, in spite of the conditions around you and the actions of others." It involves anticipating potentially dangerous situations in advance, including road conditions and errors made by other drivers, and planning how to respond to these situations. This includes constant awareness of driving conditions, planning ahead, anticipating hazards, and taking appropriate actions to prevent collisions with obstacles or other vehicles.

Question 20 - Practice Test 2

(D) When passing, maintain a safe distance from the other vehicle. Don't attempt to return to your original lane until you can see the entire front of the vehicle you just overtook in your rear-view mirror. Then, activate your turn signal, check your blind spots, and smoothly move back into the original lane.

Question 21 - Practice Test 2

(D) On highways with three or more lanes in the same direction, the middle lanes often provide the smoothest traffic flow. The left lane is primarily for drivers who wish to go faster, overtake other vehicles, or make a left turn. Slower vehicles and those intending to turn right should use the right lane.

Question 22 - Practice Test 2

(A) Your chances of survival in a car crash increase when you use both the lap and shoulder belts. The lap belt should be adjusted to fit snugly across the hips or upper thighs, never across the abdomen or soft part of the stomach. The shoulder belt should fit snugly across the chest and midpoint of the shoulder.

Question 23 - Practice Test 2

(A) When changing lanes, preparing to overtake another vehicle, or merging into traffic, signal your intentions and check for any traffic that may be passing you. Start by using your mirrors. Once your mirrors indicate it's safe to proceed, check your vehicle's blind spots by looking over your shoulder in the direction you plan to move.

Question 24 - Practice Test 2

(D) For smoother and safer driving, keep a safe distance between you and other drivers and save gas. On roadways with three or more lanes going in the same direction, the middle lanes usually offer the smoothest flow of traffic. The left lane is primarily for drivers who want to go faster, overtake, or turn left. Slower vehicles and those intending to turn right should use the right lane.

Question 25 - Practice Test 2

(A) Backing up can be dangerous because it can be difficult to see everything behind your vehicle, and other drivers typically don't expect a vehicle to be moving backward towards them. It's best to avoid backing into traffic whenever possible. However, when entering a driveway or a parallel parking space, you may need to back into it unless signs prohibit doing so. This way, when you pull out, you'll be moving forward.

Question 26 - Practice Test 2

(A) Motorcycles, like all other vehicles, need a full lane's width to maneuver safely. Therefore, you should never drive alongside a motorcycle in the same lane, even if the lane is wide and the motorcyclist is riding to one side. This is to ensure the safety of both the motorcyclist and yourself.

Question 27 - Practice Test 2

(A) Vertical rectangular signs that have black letters on a white background are typically regulatory signs. These include speed limit signs and lane usage signs, among others.

Question 28 - Practice Test 2

(D) To make a right turn, look left and right, yield the right-of-way, and hand-over-hand turn the steering wheel to complete the turn in the lane next to the curb.

Question 29 - Practice Test 2

(D) A flashing yellow traffic signal implies that you should slow down and proceed with caution. These lights are typically located at comparatively hazardous spots.

Question 30 - Practice Test 2

(A) Signs indicating construction, maintenance, or emergency operations are usually diamond-shaped or rectangular with black symbols or letters on an orange background. They serve to alert drivers that people are working in or near the roadway.

Question 31 - Practice Test 2

(D) If you experience a sudden tire blowout, firmly hold the steering wheel and gradually ease off the gas pedal. Apply gentle braking only after regaining control of your vehicle.

Question 32 - Practice Test 2

(D) Intersections are the locations where car and motorcycle accidents are most frequently encountered. This often occurs when a car driver overlooks the presence of a motorcycle and turns into its path.

Question 33 - Practice Test 2

(B) Passing is permitted when a broken line, either white or yellow, is adjacent to your lane.

Question 34 - Practice Test 2

(A) Creating a buffer of space around your vehicle, in all directions, is an effective method to prevent collisions.

Question 35 - Practice Test 2

(A) Decreasing your speed before entering a curve is advisable as braking during a curve can lead to skidding.

Question 36 - Practice Test 2

(B) When approaching a roundabout, vehicles must yield to traffic circulating the roundabout and should always enter to the right of the central island.

Question 37 - Practice Test 2

(D) In case of brake failure, remain calm. Try pumping the brake pedal unless your vehicle has ABS, which may restore some brake fluid pressure. If your vehicle has ABS, depress the brake pedal firmly. Additionally, downshift to a lower gear to use engine braking, and apply the parking brake gradually, being ready to release it to prevent skidding. As a last resort, try to slow down by brushing against something, such as a guard rail, rubbing your wheels against a curb, or driving onto a grassy area. Avoid a head-on collision at all costs as these are often fatal.

Question 38 - Practice Test 2

(A) Warning signs are generally diamond-shaped with black letters or symbols on a yellow background.

Question 39 - Practice Test 2

(B) During both day and night, large flashing or sequencing arrow panels can be used in work zones to guide drivers into specific traffic lanes and to notify them of road or street closures ahead.

Question 40 - Practice Test 2

(D) A steady yellow traffic light serves as a warning that the light will soon turn red. Prepare to stop for a red light, but avoid suddenly stopping if there's a vehicle close behind you to prevent a rear-end collision. If stopping safely isn't possible, cautiously proceed through the intersection.

PRACTICE TEST 3

Question 1 - Practice Test 3

(D) A vehicle's stopping distance is the total distance it takes to come to a complete stop. This distance is the sum of two components: the reaction distance (the distance the vehicle travels while the driver reacts and begins to apply the brakes) and the braking distance (the distance the vehicle travels while the brakes are slowing it down). Various factors, such as the vehicle's speed, the driver's alertness, and the condition of the brakes, can influence the overall stopping distance.

Question 2 - Practice Test 3

(B) When approaching a roundabout, drivers must yield the right-of-way to the traffic that is already circulating inside the roundabout. It is important to enter the roundabout on the right (counterclockwise) side, maintaining an appropriate speed.

Question 3 - Practice Test 3

(A) A double solid white line signifies that crossing over the line is prohibited and serves as a separator for lanes traveling in the same direction. Such lines are commonly used on highways to separate high-occupancy vehicle (HOV) lanes from other lanes in the same direction.

Question 4 - Practice Test 3

(B) On a one-way street with three or more lanes, drivers should use the outer lanes for turning and any lane for straight driving unless signs or road markings indicate otherwise.

Question 5 - Practice Test 3

(D) Passing is prohibited when there is a solid yellow line adjacent to your lane. It is also forbidden to pass a school bus that has activated its flashing red lights and has an extended stop arm. Additionally, passing should be avoided when approaching a hill or curve with limited visibility.

Question 6 - Practice Test 3

(D) When there are no traffic signals present, drivers must slow down or come to a stop to yield to pedestrians in marked or unmarked crosswalks. Furthermore, when making left or right turns at an intersection, it is essential to give the right-of-way to pedestrians.

Question 7 - Practice Test 3

(B) Escape ramps are specifically designed on steep mountain grades to provide a safe means of stopping runaway vehicles without jeopardizing the well-being of occupants. These ramps utilize loose, soft material, often pea gravel, to gradually slow down the vehicle.

Question 8 - Practice Test 3

(C) If a driver behind you continuously flashes their headlights, it is best to avoid any confrontations and simply move out of their way.

Question 9 - Practice Test 3

(D) Avoid attempting to overtake another vehicle when you're nearing or crossing an intersection or crosswalk.

Question 10 - Practice Test 3

(D) Contrary to the last statement, bicycles and motorcycles, being smaller and harder to spot, can move and stop faster than expected.

Question 11 - Practice Test 3

(B) If your rear wheels start to skid, turn the steering wheel in the direction the vehicle is trying to go. Steer left if your rear wheels are sliding left, and steer right if they are sliding right. The rear wheels may overcorrect and begin skidding in the opposite direction; if this happens, turn the steering wheel in that direction as well. This method, known as "steering into the skid".

Question 12 - Practice Test 3

(A) If vehicles approach an intersection from opposite directions at approximately the same time, the vehicle turning left must yield to the vehicle proceeding straight or turning right.

Question 13 - Practice Test 3

(B) Pedestrians and vehicles already in an intersection have the right-of-way. Since a roundabout or rotary is a circular intersection, you must yield the right-of-way to pedestrians and vehicles already in the circle when entering.

Question 14 - Practice Test 3

(B) High beams allow you to see further ahead, but they can create glare by reflecting off fog, rain, or snow, making it harder to see. Use low beams in fog, rain, or snow.

Question 15 - Practice Test 3

(B) You cannot pass a vehicle on the left if your lane has a solid yellow centerline. Even if your lane has a broken yellow centerline, you may not pass on the left if you would be unable to return to the right lane

Question 16 - Practice Test 3

(A) Exit ramps allow vehicles to leave expressways. Speed limits are often reduced at exit ramps.

Question 17 - Practice Test 3

(D) If the street is too narrow for a U-turn, make a three-point turn to change your vehicle's direction. This maneuver should only be performed when the street is narrow, visibility is good, traffic is light on both sides, the turn is allowed, and no other option is available.

Question 18 - Practice Test 3

(C) A single standard alcoholic drink (1.5 ounces of liquor, 5 ounces of wine, or 12 ounces of beer) can raise your blood alcohol content (BAC) to 0.02% or higher. At a BAC of 0.02%, your ability to track a moving target visually and perform two tasks simultaneously is impaired.

Question 19 - Practice Test 3

(D) When another vehicle is passing you on the left, reduce your speed slightly and maintain your position in the center of your lane until the vehicle has safely passed and is ahead of you. Once the vehicle has safely passed, you can resume your normal speed.

Question 20 - Practice Test 3

(D) When turning right on a multi-lane road, you should generally use the rightmost lane, unless signs, signals, or lane markings permit turning from multiple lanes.

Question 21 - Practice Test 3

(C) You should not pass a vehicle on the right if it is making or about to make a right turn. Ensure the passing lane is clear before attempting to pass.

Question 22 - Practice Test 3

(A) When driving in open country at night, use your high-beam headlights, as they allow you to see much further than low beams.

Question 23 - Practice Test 3

(D) Tractor-trailers often appear to be moving slower than they actually are due to their large size. Maintain a safe distance and be cautious when passing or turning around them.

Question 24 - Practice Test 3

(D) Always look both ways at railroad crossings, crosswalks, and intersections. Be sure to follow the left-right-left rule to check for approaching pedestrians, vehicles, or trains.

Question 25 - Practice Test 3

(A) You should always signal before passing another vehicle to ensure safe and clear communication with other drivers on the road.

Question 26 - Practice Test 3

(A) Your horn should be used to warn pedestrians or other drivers of potential danger. However, avoid using your horn unnecessarily or to express anger at others, as this can be a sign of aggressive driving.

Question 27 - Practice Test 3

(D) The type of alcohol does not affect your BAC, as the amount of ethanol matters rather than the form it takes. All alcoholic drinks contain different amounts of ethanol, but 1.5 ounces of 80-proof liquor, 5 ounces of wine, 12 ounces of beer, and 12 ounces of wine cooler have the same amount of ethanol.

Question 28 - Practice Test 3

(C) As the driver, you are responsible for ensuring all children in the vehicle are properly secured. Fines and penalty points may apply for each violation.

Question 29 - Practice Test 3

(C) The appropriate hand signal for a right turn is a left arm bent at 90 degrees, pointing upward.

Question 30 - Practice Test 3

(C) Treat a flashing red light like a stop sign, meaning you must stop before entering the intersection, yield to traffic and pedestrians, and proceed when safe.

Question 31 - Practice Test 3

(A) Bridges, overpasses, and ramps are especially vulnerable to icing because they are exposed to more moisture and cold air. When driving on these surfaces in freezing weather, use caution.

Question 32 - Practice Test 3

(C) Vehicles already on the expressway have the right-of-way when a vehicle is merging.

Question 33 - Practice Test 3

(C) At an all-way stop, yield to vehicles that arrived before you. Vehicles should proceed in the order they arrived, with the first vehicle to arrive going first.

Question 34 - Practice Test 3

(C) Blind pedestrians have the absolute right-of-way. Yield to the pedestrian, stopping if necessary. Avoid honking your horn near a blind pedestrian, as it may startle them or mask essential auditory cues.

Question 35 - Practice Test 3

(B) It is likely safe to merge back in front of the vehicle once you can see its entire front bumper in your rear-view mirror.

Question 36 - Practice Test 3

(A) If you're stopped at an intersection and a vehicle is rapidly approaching from behind, it's advisable to edge your vehicle forward (without entering the intersection), offering the approaching vehicle more space to halt.

Question 37 - Practice Test 3

(D) The principal aids for a blind individual are a white cane or a trained guide dog. Always yield the right-of-way to blind pedestrians.

Question 38 - Practice Test 3

(C) The total stopping distance is made up of your perception distance (the distance your vehicle travels from the time your eyes see the hazard until your brain registers it), reaction distance (the distance your vehicle travels from the time your brain tells your foot to press the brake pedal until your foot begins to brake), and braking distance (the distance your vehicle continues to travel after you've applied the brake).

Question 39 - Practice Test 3

(D) When you're at a railroad crossing with only a stop sign, you should only proceed when it's clear that no train, pedestrian, or other potential hazards are approaching, ensuring it's safe to cross.

Question 40 - Practice Test 3

(A) To prevent highway hypnosis, a state of drowsiness induced by monotonous sounds and repetitive sights, regularly shift your gaze to different parts of the road and observe various objects. Regular cell phone use or changing lanes can be risky.

ROAD SIGNS

Question 1 - Road Signs

(A) The image illustrates that overtaking on the left is permissible when the road ahead is clear. Overtaking and passing should be done with caution due to oncoming traffic.

Question 2 - Road Signs

(D) This sign denotes that a rest area is available on the right.

Question 3 - Road Signs

(C) This warning sign indicates the presence of a playground ahead.

Question 4 - Road Signs

(A) This sign warns drivers that a nearby side road crosses a railroad track. When turning onto the side road, proceed with caution.

Question 5 - Road Signs

(C) This sign denotes that you are not permitted to park in a handicap zone unless you have the necessary permit.

Question 6 - Road Signs

(C) A vehicle with a reflective triangular orange sign on the rear identifies it as a low-speed or slow-moving vehicle, which is typically defined as a motor vehicle with a top speed of no more than 25 mph. Farm vehicles and road maintenance vehicles are examples of these type of slow-moving vehicles. Slow down and proceed with caution if you come across one of these vehicles.

Question 7 - Road Signs

(B) The blue-and-white signs direct you to services such as gas stations, fast food restaurants, motels, and hospitals. Picture B indicates that there is a hospital ahead.

Question 8 - Road Signs

(C) In this case the larger sign alerts you to the impending arrival of a speed zone. The speed limit is indicated by the smaller sign. The speed limit will be reduced to 45 mph ahead in this case. So be prepared to slow down so that you don't go over the speed limit.

Question 9 - Road Signs

(A) Typically, vertical rectangular signs provide instructions or inform you of traffic laws. Drivers, pedestrians, and cyclists are given instructions by such regulatory signs.

Question 10 - Road Signs

(C) This sign denotes that the road ahead curves in the direction indicated by the arrow.

Question 11 - Road Signals Full

(A) This is a warning sign that may be placed ahead of the railroad crossing. Vehicles must slow down, look, listen, and be prepared to stop at the crossing ahead.

Question 12 - Road Signs

(A) The sequential arrow panels can be used in work zones 24 hours a day, seven days a week. This sign indicates that the lane ahead is closed and that you should take the lane to your left.

Question 13 - Road Signs

(C) This sign denotes that the divided highway is ending ahead. The road will be converted to a two-way street. Keep to the right and keep an eye out for oncoming traffic.

Question 14 - Road Signs

(B) This sign is normally displayed at an intersection with a combination of signals, including a green arrow pointing left. When the green arrow is lit, you may make a protected left turn; oncoming traffic will be stopped at a red light. This sign indicates that if the green arrow disappears and a steady green light appears, you may still make a left turn, but you must now yield to oncoming traffic before turning.

Question 15 - Road Signs

(B) A disabled crossing is indicated by the sign ahead. Slow down and take your time.

Question 16 - Road Signs

(D) This indicates a warning signal. Bicyclists and pedestrians frequently cross the road in the vicinity of the sign. You must drive cautiously and be prepared to stop.

Question 17 - Road Signs

(B) This sign denotes a bicycle crossing. This sign forewarns you that a bikeway will cross the road ahead.

Question 18 - Road Signs

(C) If you see this sign while driving in the left lane, you should turn left at the next intersection.

Question 19 - Road Signs

(D) This warning sign indicates that there will be a double curve ahead. The road ahead bends to the right, then to the left. (A winding road sign would be posted instead if there was a triple curve ahead.) Slow down, stay to the right, and do not pass.

Question 20 - Road Signs

(D) The pedestrian signals are only used to direct pedestrian traffic. This pedestrian signal indicates that pedestrians may enter the crosswalk to cross the road. (Older signals displayed the word "WALK" instead.) A signal with an upraised hand warns pedestrians not to enter the crosswalk. (Older signals displayed the words "DO NOT WALK" instead.)

Question 21 - Road Signs

(A) This navigational sign indicates the presence of a hospital ahead.

Question 22 - Road Signs

(A) This symbol indicates an exit number. This is the number assigned to a highway exit at a junction. If an interchange has more than one exit, a letter may be added to indicate which exit it is: For example: 117A, 117B, and so on.

Question 23 - Road Signs

(A) This is a gas station service sign

Question 24 - Road Signs

(C) This is a speed advisory sign at a roundabout. In the roundabout, the speed limit is 15 mph.

Question 25 - Road Signs

(A) This is a traffic control sign. This sign indicates that traffic must only make a left turn.

Question 26 - Road Signs

(A) The arrow signifies a right turn. In contrast, a red slash inside a red circle symbolizes "no." Turning right is prohibited by this regulatory sign. This sign is typically located on the right side of the road or above a driving lane.

Question 27 - Road Signs

(B) This service sign indicates that a telephone service is available ahead.

Question 28 - Road Signs

(B) This sign indicates that you need to make a right turn ahead in order to enter or stay on Interstate 95. It is guiding you to follow the direction of the arrow to continue on the correct route.

Question 29 - Road Signs

(B) This sign shows the safest speed to enter or depart an expressway. Reduce your speed to the specified speed (in this case, 30 mph).

Question 30 - Road Signs

(B) A single broken (dashed) yellow line may exist on a two-lane, two-way road. Vehicles on either side may pass if it is safe to do so.

Question 31 - Road Signs

(D) Lane use control signs are rectangular, black-and-white signs that indicate whether or not turning from specific lanes is required at an intersection. You are only permitted to drive in the direction indicated for your traffic lane.

Question 32 - Road Signs

(B) This sign shows the presence of a four-way intersection ahead. Drivers should be alert for cross traffic entering the roadway.

Question 33 - Road Signs

(A) This sign indicates a low-ground clearance railroad crossing. The railroad crossing is elevated enough that a vehicle with a large wheelbase or limited ground clearance could become stranded on the tracks. A car driver should have no trouble navigating this type of railroad crossing unless he or she is towing a trailer or driving a mobile home with low ground clearance.

Question 34 - Road Signs

(B) If your lane has a broken or dashed line (white or yellow), you may pass if it is safe to do so.

Question 35 - Road Signs

(C) A stop sign is an eight-sided white-on-red sign that indicates other traffic has the right-of-way. Always come to a complete stop before proceeding and yield to approaching vehicles.

Question 36 - Road Signs

(D) Work zone signs notify drivers of unusual or potentially hazardous conditions on or around the traveled route. These signs include black lettering or symbols on an orange background. If you encounter these signals, slow down and pay close attention.

Question 37 - Road Signs

(A) The shape of the arrow indicates that you are going to enter a winding road. A winding road has at least three turns. Take your time and slow down.

Question 38 - Road Signs

(C) When the road surface is wet, it becomes slippery. This sign is frequently found near bridges and overpasses.

Question 39 - Road Signs

(B) This is a freeway interchange sign. This sign warns you that you are approaching an interchange.

Question 40 - Road Signs

(D) This sign indicates that you must never park on the left side of the sign.

Question 41 - Road Signs

(B) This sign advises that the road ahead will be divided into two lanes. To separate opposing lanes, a divider, also known as a median, will be used. Continue right.

Question 42 - Road Signs

(B) This sign indicates that you are driving in the wrong way. Turn around.

Question 43 - Road Signs

(D) This sign denotes that the maximum nighttime speed limit is 45 mph.

Question 44 - Road Signs

(A) This is an emergency vehicle warning sign. It indicates the possibility of emergency vehicles from fire stations or other emergency facilities entering the route. If an emergency vehicle approaches from any direction and is sounding a siren, blowing an air horn, or flashing lights, you must surrender to it.

Question 45 - Road Signs

(D) This sign can be located at the end of various T-intersections. It means that before turning right or left onto the through route, you must yield the right of way or come to a complete stop.

Question 46 - Road Signs

(C) This sign indicates that U-turns are not permitted in this area.

Question 47 - Road Signs

(B) This sign indicates a T-junction. This sign indicates that the road you're on is about to come to an end. Prepare to make a right or left turn. Yield to oncoming traffic.

Question 48 - Road Signs

(A) This is an animal crossing sign. In this area, the animal represented on the sign (in this case, a deer) is common. Keep a watch out for animals like this crossing the street, particularly at dawn and night. Deer, elk, and other species roam in herds. Keep an eye out for more if you spot one. A collision with a large animal has the potential to kill the animal, do significant damage to your vehicle.

Question 49 - Road Signs

(C) This sign warns drivers not to exceed the specified speed limit in a school zone or school crossing when there are children present. In this scenario, the maximum permissible speed is 15 mph.

Question 50 - Road Signs

(B) This sign is indicating a service. It is recommended that drivers use lodging facilities if necessary.

SIGNS AND SITUATIONS

permitted to use the lane.

Question 1 - Signs & Situations

(C) When parking downhill, you should turn your front wheels toward the curb. This ensures that if your car begins to roll, the curb will stop it from moving forward. Always engage the parking brake and leave the car in the appropriate gear (Park for automatic transmissions or Reverse for manual transmissions).

Question 2 - Signs & Situations

(C) If you come to an intersection where the traffic signals are not functioning, you should treat it as if there is a stop sign at each entrance, just like a four-way stop. This means you must come to a complete stop before entering the intersection, yield to other vehicles based on standard right-of-way rules, and proceed only when it is safe to do so, exercising great caution.

Question 3 - Signs & Situations

(D) This is a reserved lane. This lane is restricted to specific types of vehicles. High-occupancy vehicle (HOV) lanes and bus lanes are two examples. Keep an eye out for signs stating which cars are

Question 4 - Signs & Situations

(C) When two vehicles approach an intersection at roughly the same moment, the vehicle on the left must yield to the one on the right. In the absence of this rule, the vehicle turning left must yield to approaching traffic. Car A must yield to Car B in this situation.

Question 5 - Signs & Situations

(A) If your brakes fail while driving downhill, the vehicle may begin to roll forward. You can configure the transmission to counteract this movement. Set your manual transmission to Reverse. Set the automatic transmission to Park if you have one.

Question 6 - Signs & Situations

(C) At an uncontrolled intersection, a vehicle must yield to pedestrians in a marked or unmarked crosswalk. After considering pedestrians, each vehicle must yield to the one on its right. Consequently, Vehicle C must yield to Vehicle B, and Vehicle A must yield to Vehicle C.

Question 7 - Signs & Situations

(D) Lane use control signals are special overhead signals that indicate which lanes of a roadway may be utilized in various directions at different times. A flashing yellow "X" denotes that this lane is solely for left turns.

Question 8 - Signs & Situations

(C) If your vehicle's brakes fail while parked uphill, it may start rolling backward. To counter this movement, set your transmission accordingly. For manual transmissions, set it to first gear for maximum forward torque. For automatic transmissions, set it to Park.

Question 9 - Signs & Situations

(B) Always follow directions from a police officer, even if it means disregarding other traffic devices or rules. For example, drive through a red light or stop sign if a police officer waves you through.

Question 10 - Signs & Situations

(B) Consider a flashing red signal to be a STOP sign. That is, you must come to a complete stop before crossing the intersection, yield to oncoming vehicles and pedestrians, and then proceed cautiously when it is safe to do so.

Question 11 - Signs & Situations

(C) This sign suggests that the recommended speed for navigating the upcoming curve is 35 mph. The sign does not provide any details regarding the curve's angle.

Question 12 - Signs & Situations

(A) You must come to a complete stop and yield to all traffic and pedestrians ahead. You can then proceed when the intersection is clear and there are no vehicles approaching that may present a hazard.

Question 13 - Signs & Situations

(A) High-occupancy vehicle (HOV) lanes are designed for vehicles with multiple occupants. This sign means that this lane is an HOV 2+ lane, which requires at least two occupants in each vehicle. In other words, a driver and at least one passenger. An HOV 3+ lane would require a driver and at least two passengers.

Question 14 - Signs & Situations

(A) When two vehicles arrive at an uncontrolled intersection about the same time, the vehicle on the left must yield. Car A must yield in this situation.

Question 15 - Signs & Situations

(C) After yielding to all pedestrians and vehicles already in the junction, you can proceed on a green signal.

Question 16 - Signs & Situations

(A) If you have a green light, you may continue through the intersection, but you must first yield to all pedestrians and vehicles already in the intersection. In this case, Car A must yield to Car B since Car B has already entered the intersection.

Question 17 - Signs & Situations

(C) Prior to making a left turn off the road, you must yield to all pedestrians and oncoming traffic.

Question 18 - Signs & Situations

(D) Roads are typically at their slipperiest during the first 30 minutes of rain because the water mixes with dirt, oil, and other substances on the road, creating a slick surface. This condition will persist until more rain washes away these materials. Additionally, using cruise control on wet, icy, or snowy roads can be dangerous because it may cause your vehicle to lose traction, increasing the risk of a skid.

Question 19 - Signs & Situations

(D) At a STOP sign, you must stop before the stop line. If there isn't a stop line, stop before the crosswalk. If there isn't a crosswalk either, stop before entering the intersection.

Question 20 - Signs & Situations

(B) You may turn left on a green light after yielding to pedestrians, oncoming vehicles, and vehicles already in the intersection.

Question 21 - Signs & Situations

(A) When parking uphill parallel to a curb, point your wheels away from the curb and allow your vehicle to roll back slightly so the rear part of the front wheel on the curb side rests against the curb. If your brakes fail, the curb will prevent your car from rolling backward. Ensure you still engage your parking brake and leave your car in the appropriate gear.

Question 22 - Signs & Situations

(A) The sign displayed is a yield sign. When you encounter a yield sign, you should slow down and be ready to yield to both pedestrians and oncoming traffic. It's important to note that you may need to stop if there are pedestrians or vehicles that have the right of way.

Question 23 - Signs & Situations

(A) The driver intends to turn left.

Question 24 - Signs & Situations

(A) A flashing yellow traffic signal means that you should slow down and proceed with caution.

Question 25 - Signs & Situations

(C) If your turn signals and brake lights aren't working, try hand and arm signals. An arm pointing downward is a signal to slow down or stop.

FINE & LIMITS

Question 1 - Fines & Limits

(D) If you do not uphold the required auto insurance coverage in Illinois, you'll be subjected to a fine, suspension of your driving license and your vehicle's registration until proof of insurance is furnished.

Question 2 - Fines & Limits

(C) In Illinois, when you're operating a vehicle, you're implicitly granting permission to law enforcement to test you for the presence of controlled substances.

Question 3 - Fines & Limits

(C) An Occupational Driving Permit (ODP) in Illinois allows a professional driver, whose license has been suspended due to three moving violations, to continue driving for job-related purposes.

Question 4 - Fines & Limits

(B) In Illinois, if a driver under 21 years of age is found guilty of two or more moving violations within a two-year period, their license will be suspended for a minimum of 30 days.

Question 5 - Fines & Limits

(B) Upon a DUI arrest in Illinois, your license will be taken by the officer, but you'll receive a temporary receipt that enables you to continue driving for 45 days, until the suspension starts on the 46th day.

Question 6 - Fines & Limits

(D) Passengers in chartered buses, motor homes, and limousines are exceptions to the Illinois law that prohibits drinking in vehicles.

Question 7 - Fines & Limits

(A) In Illinois, a 16-year-old driver can apply for a standard driver's license after holding a valid instruction permit for 9 months.

Question 8 - Fines & Limits

(D) If a driver is arrested in Illinois for driving with a BAC of 0.08% or higher, their license will be suspended for at least 6 months.

Question 9 - Fines & Limits

(C) If an underage driver in Illinois is placed under court supervision due to an alcohol-related offense, their driver's license will be suspended for three months.

Question 10 - Fines & Limits

(D) The safety belt law in Illinois mandates that all passengers 8 years or older in a vehicle wear seat belts. Those below the age of 8 must be secured in an appropriate child restraint.

DISTRACTED DRIVING

Question 1 - Distracted Driving

(B) It is preferable to use a hands-free or speaker phone while driving if you are an adult driver and absolutely must use your phone. In several states, it is illegal and not advised to use a mobile phone while driving.

Question 2 - Distracted Driving

(C) Never turn around to attend to the needs of passengers, kids, or animals while you are driving. Pull over to the side of the road and park your vehicle if you need to attend to any passengers or animals.

Question 3 - Distracted Driving

(A) Although stimulants, physical activity, and music can help you stay alert, sleeping is the greatest cure for fatigue. Consult a doctor if, despite receiving 9 hours of sleep, you still feel exhausted.

Question 4 - Distracted Driving

(D) Before taking a medication, look for any warnings about its effect(s) while you are driving. Ask your doctor or pharmacist about any potential side effects if you are unsure if it is safe to take the medication and drive. Drugs used to treat headaches, colds, hay fever or other allergies, or to calm nerves might cause drowsiness and have an impact on a person's ability to drive. Similar to how alcohol does, some prescription medications can impair your reflexes, judgment, eyesight, and awareness.

Question 5 - Distracted Driving

(C) Many over-the-counter and prescription drugs might make you sleepy. Only use drugs while driving if your doctor says they won't impair your ability to drive safely.

Question 6 - Distracted Driving

(D) Texting while driving currently accounts for 25% of all car accidents in the US and is the greatest cause of death for youths. Texting while driving is illegal.

Question 7 - Distracted Driving

(A) Talking on a cell phone while driving increases your chances of being in a crash by up to four times. This is because the talk is taking your focus away from driving. Sending text messages (texting) while driving increases your chances of being in an accident by up to eightfold.

Question 8 - Distracted Driving

(D) Cell phones are not permitted to be used by underage drivers while driving, unless to notify an emergency.

Question 9 - Distracted Driving

(D) Distractions, even on straight roads or empty roads, should be avoided. Refrain from eating, drinking, smoking, texting, reading, or engaging in difficult conversations while driving. If possible, turn off your phone and keep it off until you have completed driving for the day.

Question 10 - Distracted Driving

(D) Fatigue can impair your judgment, slow down your reaction times, and decrease your awareness of your surroundings.

Question 11 - Distracted Driving

(D) Distractions while driving include text messaging, talking on the phone, dealing with children, and lighting a cigarette, among other activities that draw your attention away from the road.

Question 12 - Distracted Driving

(D) It is risky to do anything while driving that diverts your attention from the road, including getting dressed, putting on makeup, reading, eating, or drinking. Take care not to hold someone in your lap, or a pet or parcel in your arms.

Question 13 - Distracted Driving

(B) Highway hypnosis or drowsiness while driving can result from monotonous road and traffic conditions, the hum of wind, tires, and the engine. Drivers can avoid highway hypnosis by continuously moving their eyes and monitoring traffic and road signs around them.

Question 14 - Distracted Driving

(D) Activities that require the use of your hands should be avoided while driving. Listening to the radio, however, can help you stay alert.

Question 15 - Distracted Driving

(B) It is against the law for minors to use a cell phone while driving. If a cell phone rings, they should not answer the call. Violators of this law may face fines.

Question 16 - Distracted Driving

(C) You should set up your cab before starting your trip, but eating and drinking should be done at rest stops.

Question 17 - Distracted Driving

(A) Driving while operating a visual screen device or texting is illegal and prohibited by law.

Question 18 - Distracted Driving

(D) You should also be aware of potential distractions and impairments, as they can affect your driving abilities. All the listed factors, including emotional and physical states like fatigue, anger, illness, stress, and fear, can impair your driving skills.

DRINKING AND DRIVING

Question 1 - Drinking and Driving

(A) You should arrange for a designated driver to take you home if you've consumed too much alcohol to drive safely. A designated driver is someone who abstains from drinking and is responsible for driving others who have been drinking.

Question 2 - Drinking and Driving

(A) Only time can effectively eliminate alcohol from a person's system. Coffee and fresh air might alleviate some symptoms of intoxication but will not reduce the actual level of impairment.

Question 3 - Drinking and Driving

(D) Upon conviction of driving under the influence of alcohol or drugs, penalties may include license suspension, significant fines, and community service.

Question 4 - Drinking and Driving

(A) Alcohol consumption impairs vision, slows reactions, and affects judgment but does not increase alertness.

Question 5 - Drinking and Driving

(D) A standard serving of alcohol is typically 1.5 ounces, regardless of the type of drink.

Question 6 - Drinking and Driving

(C) Drinking alcohol and driving at night is especially risky because vision is already restricted due to darkness.

Question 7 - Drinking and Driving

(D) The type of alcohol does not affect blood alcohol concentration, as standard servings of different types of alcohol contain the same amount of alcohol.

Question 8 - Drinking and Driving

(D) Even small amounts of alcohol can impair a driver's reflexes, driving skills, and depth perception.

Question 9 - Drinking and Driving

(D) License suspension is mandatory for minors convicted of driving under the influence of drugs or transporting an open container of any alcoholic beverage.

Question 10 - Drinking and Driving

(B) Drunk driving is the leading cause of death among young Americans aged 16 to 24, with alcohol-related crashes occurring every 33 minutes.

Question 11 - Drinking and Driving

(D) Open containers of alcohol are only allowed in areas inaccessible to drivers or passengers, such as trunks, cargo areas, or truck beds.

Question 12 - Drinking and Driving

(D) Alcohol can impact your concentration, reaction time, and judgment.

Question 13 - Drinking and Driving

(D) Consuming alcohol before or while driving can diminish a driver's reflexes, physical control of the vehicle, and awareness of potential dangers on the road.

Question 14 - Drinking and Driving

(A) Drivers under 21 are not permitted to buy, consume, or possess alcohol.

Question 15 - Drinking and Driving

(A) The liver can process approximately one standard drink per hour. If you consume a large amount of alcohol, it may take a day or two for your body to fully recover.

Question 16 - Drinking and Driving

(A) Open container laws prohibit open containers of alcohol in areas accessible to the driver or passengers of a vehicle, with exceptions for limousines, taxis, motor homes, and commercial buses.

Question 17 - Drinking and Driving

(D) If you plan to drink alcohol, consider using public transportation, a taxi, or designating a sober driver to get home safely.

Question 18 - Drinking and Driving

(D) Drivers under the influence of alcohol are more likely to drive too fast or too slow, change lanes frequently, and fail to dim headlights.

Question 19 - Drinking and Driving

(D) Alcohol enters the bloodstream and affects various bodily processes, such as coordination, self-control, and reaction time. The only way to counteract alcohol's impact on the brain is to wait for it to leave the bloodstream.

Question 20 - Drinking and Driving

(A) The amount of alcohol a person can consume before reaching the legal limit varies from one individual to another and is influenced by several factors, such as body weight, metabolism, and tolerance.

MOCK TEST PRACTICE

.

Question 1 - Mock Exam

(C) Speed limit signs and advisory (recommended) speed signs are the two types of speed signs. Speed limit signs display the legal permitted limits in black characters and digits on a rectangular white background. Advisory speed signs have black letters on a yellow backdrop and are frequently put in conjunction with a warning sign. In contrast to speed limits, recommended speeds are rarely enforced. However, if you exceed the advisory speed and cause an accident, you may face penalties.

Question 2 - Mock Exam

(A) If a railroad crossing lacks warning devices or only displays a crossbuck sign, you should slow down and watch and listen for a train before moving forward. Any approaching train has the right of way that you must yield to.

Question 3 - Mock Exam

(C) If traffic from a different road is merging onto your road, you should alter your speed and vehicle position to allow the traffic to merge safely.

Question 4 - Mock Exam

(D) Stay vigilant for cyclists on the road, as they can be hard to spot. When overtaking a bicycle moving in the same direction, you must maintain a minimum safe distance of 3 feet.

Question 5 - Mock Exam

(B) Avoid parking your vehicle on the railroad tracks, which is obviously dangerous. At a railroad crossing, wait until there's enough space for your vehicle on the other side before crossing. Always yield to the train as it cannot stop for you. As you cross, avoid changing gears as this could cause your vehicle to stall on the tracks.

Question 6 - Mock Exam

(D) Median crossovers are legally intended only for authorized vehicles, such as emergency and maintenance vehicles.

Question 7 - Mock Exam

(D) While driving in the city, to prevent sudden braking or a need to turn abruptly, it's best to scan the road at least ten seconds ahead of your vehicle. This precaution gives you more time to react to potential hazards, enabling safer driving, fuel efficiency, and straighter steering.

Question 8 - Mock Exam

(A) The outer edges of many roadways are marked with a solid white line. This line defines the outer edge of the roadway and can only be crossed by traffic moving to or from the shoulder. On divided roadways, the "inner edges" (i.e., the divider between the left lane and the center) are marked with a solid yellow line.

Question 9 - Mock Exam

(A) When approaching a STOP sign, you are required to stop at the solid white stop line or parallel to the stop sign. If a stop line is absent, stop before entering the crosswalk on your side of the intersection.

Question 10 - Mock Exam

(B) If an emergency vehicle approaches while you are in an intersection, continue through the intersection. Once through, pull over to the right as soon as possible and stop.

Question 11 - Mock Exam

(A) Crosswalk lines are pairs of longitudinal white lines that delineate where pedestrians are permitted to walk. Blocking these with your vehicle is prohibited.

Question 12 - Mock Exam

(B) While driving down a steep hill, the appropriate action is to release the accelerator pedal and shift into a lower gear. Using engine braking can help control the vehicle's speed without causing brake fade from overuse of brakes.

Question 13 - Mock Exam

(C) When a vehicle is passing you on the left side, refrain from increasing your speed. Allow the other vehicle to overtake you safely.

Question 14 - Mock Exam

(D) In situations where you have the right of way at an intersection but a pedestrian begins crossing against a red light, your initial reaction should be to sound your horn to alert them. If the pedestrian continues, you should stop your vehicle.

Question 15 - Mock Exam

(A) In the absence of any specific reduced speed limit signs at work zones, you should adhere to the regular posted speed limit.

Question 16 - Mock Exam

(C) For making a left turn from a two-way street onto a one-way street, position your vehicle such that your left wheels are as close as possible to the yellow dividing line.

Question 17 - Mock Exam

(A) Before making a right turn, it's important to avoid swinging wide to the left as it can confuse drivers behind you, who might think you're turning left or changing lanes.

Question 18 - Mock Exam

(B) An acceleration lane is typically found at the end of most freeway on-ramps, allowing you to increase your speed to match the freeway traffic.

Question 19 - Mock Exam

(B) Before changing lanes, ensure to check your mirrors for any vehicles and also look over your shoulder to the rear to spot any vehicles in your blind spot.

Question 20 - Mock Exam

(A) When passing a larger vehicle, it's safe to merge back into the lane once you can clearly see the vehicle's headlights in your rear-view mirror. Large vehicles require a longer stopping distance, so ensuring a safe gap is crucial.

Question 21 - Mock Exam

(B) Contrary to common belief, bicycles and motorcycles are not only smaller and harder to spot than cars or trucks, but they can also maneuver and stop more quickly than expected.

Question 22 - Mock Exam

(C) You should adjust your driving to account for the weather. Slow down and increase your following distance when the weather is bad. Conditions like rain, snow, and ice can limit your visibility and increase the distance you need to stop your vehicle safely. So, you should start braking earlier and more gently than usual in these situations.

Question 23 - Mock Exam

(C) At night, if you're following another vehicle, it's recommended to dim your high-beam headlights. Bright lights can temporarily blind the driver in front of you as they reflect off the vehicle's rearview mirrors.

Question 24 - Mock Exam

(A) When you plan to make a right turn at an intersection, you should stay as close to the right as possible. Execute the turn near the right curb to avoid crossing into other traffic lanes.

Question 25 - Mock Exam

(A) To integrate seamlessly into freeway traffic from an entry ramp or acceleration lane, one must bring their speed up to match that of the vehicles in the right lane. Afterward, indicate your intent to merge, verify the conditions around you, and then merge with caution.

Question 26 - Mock Exam

(D) In a skid, the most critical piece of vehicle control equipment to employ is the steering wheel. If your back wheels start skidding to the left, steer left; if they begin skidding to the right, steer right. Once you sense that the vehicle is back under your control, align the front wheels.

Question 27 - Mock Exam

(B) Double solid yellow lines in the middle of the roadway are used to indicate the center of a roadway where there are four or more lanes of traffic moving in opposite directions. These lines can only be crossed to make a left turn into or from an alley, private road, or driveway.

Question 28 - Mock Exam

(C) In the event of having to park on a roadway, always position your vehicle as far from traffic as you can. If there is a curb present, park as near to it as possible.

Question 29 - Mock Exam

(D) High beams should be used on unfamiliar roads, in construction zones, or in areas where people might be on the side of the road and where there are no oncoming vehicles. High beams provide twice the visibility range of low beams.

Question 30 - Mock Exam

(D) Driving on the left side of the road is only legal under certain circumstances, such as on one-way streets and when overtaking another vehicle. On a multilane highway, you are required to drive on the right half of the road unless you are overtaking another vehicle, making a left turn, or avoiding an obstacle.

Question 31 - Mock Exam

(D) A roundabout is a circular junction where traffic moves in a counterclockwise direction around a central island. As you enter a roundabout, keep to the right of the central island. Don't stop if the way is clear. Never pass or overtake another vehicle in a single-lane roundabout. Continue around the circle until you reach your exit, then signal right and leave the roundabout.

Question 32 - Mock Exam

(C) If a U-turn cannot be performed due to space limitations, consider a three-point turn instead. Both maneuvers will result in your vehicle facing in the opposite direction. Three-point turns can only be made when the street is narrow, visibility is good, traffic is light, the turn is permitted, and there's no better alternative.

Question 33 - Mock Exam

(A) A U-turn should only be performed when it is safe. Avoid executing a U-turn on a bend or near the crest of a hill as your vehicle may be hidden from other drivers. You should never make a U-turn at a location marked with a "No U-Turn" sign. Also, refrain from making a U-turn at a traffic signal-controlled intersection or in front of a police officer.

Question 34 - Mock Exam

(A) A flashing yellow traffic signal necessitates that you slow down and proceed with caution, not a complete stop.

Question 35 - Mock Exam

(A) If there are vehicles following you when you exit a high-speed, two-lane roadway, you should not decelerate suddenly. A sudden drop in speed may cause the following vehicle to collide with yours.

Made in the USA
Monee, IL
25 June 2025

20005235R00105